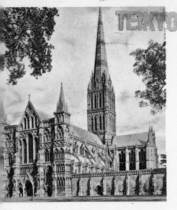

For more than a thousand years the Byzantine Empire preserved and extended the treasures of Christian civilization. Today its artistic glories lie scattered through many lands, and it is not easy to obtain an accurate and comprehensive picture of its rich traditions. For this task no better authority could have been found than Professor André Grabar, the internationally famous Byzantinist, and member of the Collège de France. In this addition to the ART OF THE WORLD series, he concentrates on the medieval period, from the Iconoclast emperors in the eighth century to the fall of Constantinople in 1453. The first part of his text contains an analytical survey of the principal problems involved. The second gives a detailed appreciation by periods of the Empire's achievements in architecture, mosaic, painting, sculpture, manuscript illustration, and other arts. Due attention is paid to the techniques involved, as well as to the esthetic value of the works under discussion. Professor Grabar shows how Byzantine churches and their decoration served to express in symbolic form the religious world picture of those who worshipped in them, and throws light on the parallels and contrasts beween Byzantine art and that of the medieval West. The examples he quotes are drawn not only from Constantinople itself but also from Greece, the Balkans, and less familiar parts of the Empire.

With 57 color plates, 14 black-and-white plates, map, and chronological tables.

GIFT OF

DR. ROBERT HERRICK

THE ART OF THE
BYZANTINE EMPIRE

BYZANTINE ART IN THE MIDDLE AGES

ANDRÉ GRABAR

GREYSTONE PRESS/NEW YORK

Translated by Betty Forster

Frontispiece: *Christ Pantocrator.*
Mosaic in the dome of the cathedral at Arta in Epirus, ca. 1300.

REVISED EDITION 1967
© 1963 BY HOLLE VERLAG G.M.B.H., BADEN-BADEN, GERMANY
LIBRARY OF CONGRESS CATALOG CARD NUMBER: 66–21147
MANUFACTURED IN THE UNITED STATES OF AMERICA

CONTENTS

LIST OF PLATES

LIST OF PLANS

MAP

6

ACKNOWLEDGEMENTS

The following libraries and museums kindly allowed reproduction of the works represented in the plates on the following pages:

Bibliothèque Nationale, Paris   21, 41, 42, 43, 69, 88, 118, 136, 138, 141, 142

Byzantine Museum, Athens   186

Cabinet des Médailles, Paris   45, 159

Laurentian Library, Florence   65, 139

Marcian Library, Venice   67, 162

Museo Sacro, Vatican   184

National Library, Vienna   20

Palatine Library, Parma   140

Treasury of St. Mark's, Venice   19, 44, 68, 160

Vatican Library   64, 135, 137

The plates on the following pages were taken and kindly made available by:

Mme. Florand   Frontispiece, 39, 40, 63, 66, 70, 89, 90, 91, 93, 111, 113, 114, 115

Mme. Hassia   185, 186

J. Powell   92, 112, 164, 165, 166, 183

M. and Mme. Thierry   22, 87, 116

The other plates, taken by Mlle. D. Fourmont, belong to the Ecole des Hautes Etudes, Paris.

The plans were kindly drawn by M. A. Khatchatrian.

TRANSLATOR'S NOTE

In the spelling of names Latinized forms have generally been preferred to those from the Greek.

THE BYZANTINE EMPIRE IN THE MIDDLE AGES

Mesembria

BLACK SEA

Trebizond

ple

Nicaea

hesus

Caesarea

CAPPADOCIA

CILICIA

Rhodes

CYPRUS

PART I

GENERAL CHARACTERISTICS OF
BYZANTINE ART

I. THE GEOGRAPHICAL
AND HISTORICAL FRAMEWORK

The aim of this book is to present and study Byzantine medieval art, the origins of which go back to the Iconoclasts (762–843), and which in principle stops with the fall of the East Christian Empire and the capture of Constantinople by the Turks in 1543.

It is evident that these limits are somewhat theoretical. There were, before the year 726, works of Byzantine art which heralded the Middle Ages — and the disappearance of the Byzantine state in 1453 did not mean that at that date all artistic activity faithful to the Byzantine tradition ceased. We shall often be writing of the Byzantine traditions established before the Iconoclast period which maintained and renewed themselves during the period we are to study. It seems useful to state from the beginning that the history of Byzantine art during the period which stretches from the end of antiquity to the eve of modern times presents a far greater continuity than the history of Western art during the same period. We will explain later the reasons for this continuity. Nevertheless in Byzantium, as in the West, art as practised during the Middle Ages had its own characteristics, which it is useful and fair to separate from those of the art which was practised previously — between the reign of Constantine, who founded Constantinople in 330, and the beginnings of the Iconoclast crisis (330–726). It is entirely to medieval art that we are going to devote ourselves, returning to its origins only where it may help us to a better understanding of medieval Byzantine works and the artistic life of Constantinople during the Middle Ages.

Individuality of medieval Byzantine art

When one tries to imagine the territory over which the artistic works of the Byzantines stretched during the period we are studying, one naturally thinks of Constantinople, of Greece with its islands, and of the whole of the Mediterranean provinces around the capital on the Bosphorus. This summary description of the area in which Byzantine artists were active is not false, but it requires more precise definition. One must above all remember the essential fact that

Geographical spread of Byzantine art

Byzantine territory itself and that of the area it influenced in matters of art and culture did not remain the same between 726 and 1453. From the end of antiquity to the period of the foundation of Constantinople, and again in the sixth century under Justinian and his successors, the art which was to remain the basis of Byzantine art was practised, with fairly evident regional differences, in the *Successive* whole eastern half of the Roman Empire, which then stretched as *reductions of* far as the Euphrates and upper Mesopotamia, and as far as the *Byzantine Empire* Nubian desert in Egypt. The Arab conquest in the seventh century removed Egypt, Syria and a part of Asia Minor so that the Byzantine Empire was reduced by half and came to be concentrated around the Greek lands. It then became definitely hellenized and kept to the very end that ethnic and cultural predominance of things Greek, to the detriment of the Latin element which the Roman conquests had established everywhere around the Mediterranean. It also discarded the Semitic elements which, after the annexation of the countries of the Levant by Rome, had played an active part in the development of the empire.

While the Arabs seized from Byzantium her rich provinces in the Levant, the Lombards reduced her Italian possessions and the Bulgars crossed the Danube and settled in the north-eastern Balkans, where Slav infiltration spread progressively, reaching the shores of Salonika (Thessalonica) and the core of the oldest Greek provinces. At times Arabs, Khazars, and Bulgarians ventured as far as the gates of Constantinople and endangered the very existence of the Byzantine state. The historical role of the emperors of the eighth and *The 'Iconoclast'* the beginning of the ninth centuries was to have stopped these in-*emperors* vasions, and to have ensured the survival of the Christian empire of Byzantium. The attack against images which they launched at the same time, undoubtedly with military reasons in mind (in order to ensure the active participation of the Christians of eastern Asia Minor — a frontier district, where the fate of the empire was at stake), earned them the title of Iconoclasts. This sobriquet, although a questionable one if we take into consideration the whole of their work, does however describe one particular aspect of their reign — their religious and artistic activities. We shall return to this point, only observing in passing their opposition as emperors to images —

an attitude taken up in defence of Byzantine territory at the period when it was most reduced.

Their military successes, which were continued and increased during the rule of the Amorian (820–867) and particularly the Macedonian dynasty (867–1056), gave back to Byzantium a political stability which she was losing, and at the same time remarkable economic strength and great international prestige. For several centuries the empire of Constantinople again became the most important power in the Mediterranean world; but its territory was not significantly increased as compared with the Iconoclast period. There were of course brilliant reconquests in the tenth century, some temporary, others permanent, in the direction of Armenia, Syria and even Palestine, under Nicephorus Phocas and John Tzimisces, and other reconquests at the beginning of the eleventh century towards Bulgaria, Dalmatia and even southern Italy. But these territorial extensions of the empire — which play a part in the history of art through Byzantine institutions in these territories being brought back to the mother country — were not to be maintained. A terrible defeat of the Byzantine armies by the Turks in 1071 and the development of the Slav kingdoms in the Balkans in the twelfth century prevented Byzantium from holding on to them. So one can say that, from the fall of the Iconoclasts (843) to the end of the twelfth century, the area of Byzantine expansion remained essentially the same. Roughly speaking, it included on one hand all the territory between Dalmatia and the lower Danube, and on the other the southern extremity of the Greek archipelago, as well as the western part of Asia Minor and its coastal regions, up to and including Trebizond in the north and Antioch in the south.

During the twelfth century the territorial problems of the Byzantine state became complicated by frequent campaigns against the Serbian and particularly Norman kings, and by the Crusaders crossing and sometimes fighting their way through the countries of the Byzantine empire. They even carved out for themselves fiefs in the Antioch area, whereas the Armenian princes, who had taken refuge from the Turks, made of the Byzantine province of Cilicia a 'little Armenia'. But for the study of art the passage to and fro of foreign armies, the political insecurity, and the more or less short-

Amorian and Macedonian dynasties

Territories of the Byzantine Empire from the Xth to the XIIth century

lived changes in sovereignty which they brought about in one or other of the frontier provinces, are of little importance. For in all these territories within the area just described, quite independently of the politico-geographical fluctuations, it was the same Byzantine art that was invariably practised, whether it was executed by the Byzantines themselves or by those who tried, and often succeeded, in displacing them politically from these provinces.

Extension of Byzantine arts beyond political frontiers

In other words, from the point of view of artistic geography, Byzantium enjoyed such a true predominance in culture and in technical skills, and such prestige in the artistic field, that the area of its artistic expansion spread constantly beyond the frontiers of the Byzantine state. The main agents of this expansion were the Greek Christians established in foreign countries — and the foreign Christians converted by Byzantine missions. This was the case in Syria, Armenia and southern Italy on one hand, and in Georgia and the Slav countries on the other. The mission to the Slavs was particularly fruitful from this point of view. If politically, during the period under review, the territory of the Byzantine Empire increased only occasionally and then for a short time, it did however undergo an extraordinary expansion between the end of the ninth and the end of the tenth centuries, following the religious conquest of all the Balkan countries, and of the whole of Russia. This time it was the field of religious (not political) conquest which served as a background to the widespread influence of art. If there is one sphere where the progress of Byzantium is a reality, and compensates for so many territorial withdrawals since the seventh century, it is in the

Influences of religious conquest on spread of art

field of art. From the ninth century onwards the Orthodox religion, directed with a firm hand by the Church of Constantinople, was an important vehicle in the spreading of this art beyond the borders of the Byzantine state. It was to continue to play this role, even to an enhanced extent, during the periods when the political power of the Byzantine state suffered an eclipse.

We must here note this fact, which is an important one for appreciating the exceptional part played by Byzantine art in the Middle Ages. But in this book we shall only concern ourselves with truly Byzantine works, reserving the study of art in the different countries of Eastern Europe for another volume in this series.

It is from the twelfth century onwards that one witnesses the divorce between the Byzantine state and the art which it had promoted, the immense territorial extent of the latter having no common measure with the very reduced territory of the empire under the Comneni and the Angeli (1081–1185, 1185–1204). Admittedly it was the Comneni who reconquered the easternmost part of the southern coast of Asia Minor, as far as and including Antioch. But this modest increase in imperial territory did not spread beyond the districts of neighbouring Cappadocia, where however the execution of art in the Byzantine tradition continued even though the country was part of the Turkish sultanate of Iconium.

The Comneni and the Angeli

In 1204, diverted from its real aim, the Fourth Crusade took Constantinople and devastated it. While the Byzantine state, Greek and Orthodox, reconstituted itself on the Asiatic coast of the Bosphorus around the city of Nicaea, the conquerors of 1204 attempted to found a Latin and Catholic empire based on Constantinople. This state, organized on the Western pattern of the period, was bordered by a series of feudal principalities covering practically the whole territory of continental Greece and its islands; it did not resist long attempts at reconquest led by the exiled Greek emperors in Nicaea.

Fourth Crusade

In 1261 the latter returned to Constantinople, reconstituting the link with the Byzantine past. We know practically nothing of Greek artistic activities during the Latin Empire. This is perhaps due in part to the accidental destruction of works of art which date from that half-century. One may of course ask oneself whether an art, which at that period was exclusively religious, must not have been dimmed by the brutal installation of the Latin clergy in Constantinople and the forced withdrawal of the Greek clergy and of those who, by the means at their disposal and their influence, were the traditional patrons of Byzantine artistic works — that is to say, the emperors and the aristocracy of Byzantium. The Latin domination, which in Constantinople and its district lasted for half a century and even longer in certain parts of Greece and in the islands, left remarkably few traces of monuments. This fact is very striking when one thinks of the considerable and simultaneous expansion of

Reconquest of Constantinople by emperors of Nicaea

Western art in the Holy Land. Although this question has never been studied, it is worth bearing in mind. The lack of Latin activity in the field of art in the truly Greek countries is probably due to several causes. The absence of powerful opponents in the district made the building of a great number of fortified castles and other military works unnecessary; the small number of Latin residents did not encourage the founding of more churches; but above all, contrary to their experience in the Levant, the Crusaders found on the spot numbers of ready-made churches of which they made use to practise their religion, after removing the Greek clergy. It was only in places where the power of the Western states or that of their princes lasted much longer, as in the islands seized by the Venetians (i.e., the Ionian Islands, Crete and Rhodes), or by the Genoese (Chios), or in Cyprus where Lusignan kings reigned that the contribution of European art was felt — at least in certain fields, and particularly in military and religious architecture. As far as the rest is concerned the loss of Greek sovereignty in these territories did not bring about a new artistic orientation. Thus here, too, the prestige of the Byzantine tradition worked with success — all the more so as the population, which was Greek and Orthodox, continued to belong to their Church.

Even more strongly was the Byzantine artistic tradition able to perpetuate itself in all those more or less independent small states of the empire of Constantinople, even when the princes who reigned there were momentarily at war with the Byzantine emperors. This was to be seen in the Morea, Epirus and in Macedonia where the population was either Greek or hellenized and Orthodox. The princes of these states, which lasted for varying lengths of time (such as Serbia and Bulgaria, which had re-formed or consolidated their power in the thirteenth century and were to disintegrate under the continued blows of the Turks a hundred or a hundred and fifty years later), everywhere exercised an influence favourable to the extension or maintenance of Byzantine artistic tradition; for these potentates dreamt either of usurping the power of the emperors in Constantinople itself or of imitating them within the boundaries of their own possessions. In both cases Byzantine art was part of the show of imperial tradition it was necessary to display.

Maintenance of Byzantine artistic tradition under Latin domination

Influence of Byzantine art on art of Orthodox countries

PLATE I – Two military saints. Detail of an icon, XIth-century enamel. *Treasury of St. Mark's, Venice.*
Cf. p. 34

PLATE 2 – Portrait of the Emperor Alexius v Murtzuphlus. Miniature, *ca.* 1200. *National Library, Vienna (Cod. Hist. Gr. 53). Cf. p. 36*

PLATE 3 – Council of the Byzantine Church at Constantinople in 1351. Detail from a miniature. *Bibliothèque Nationale, Paris (Cod. Gr. 1242). Cf. p. 62*

PLATE 4 – Descent into Limbo. xɪth-century mural painting in the rock-cut chapel of St. Barbara of Soganli, Cappadocia. *Cf. p. 26*

In other words, during this last period of the Byzantine state, when the name of empire was only given to Constantinople and its suburbs, Byzantine art continued to flourish in all the territories which, whatever the race, language or creed of their inhabitants, were governed by Christian potentates. This flowering was complete where the Orthodox religion predominated. Also, whereas during the period from the ninth to the eleventh century the conquest of new territories by Byzantine art was mainly accomplished through missionaries, behind whom often stood the government of Byzantium, during the Palaeologian period this part was reserved to the slow action of frequent contacts between Greeks and Latins, Greeks and Slavs, Rumanians, Georgians. All these foreigners had been able to see for themselves innumerable works of Byzantine art in the countries where that art was traditionally practised. As for the Western world, it was the technical, aesthetic and religious qualities of Byzantine works which alone were responsible for the great *Influence of Byzantine* movement to the West of Byzantine works of art and for their *art on the West* imitation everywhere in Europe, from Italy to England, in the tenth and eleventh centuries, and particularly at the end of the twelfth and in the thirteenth century. As an Italian art historian said recently, during the thirteenth century every Italian artist had personal experience of Byzantine art.

In short, during this late period (thirteenth to fifteenth century) Byzantine art, in an even more spectacular fashion than in the past, spread beyond the frontiers of the small state which continued to be called the Byzantine Empire. However, this drive towards the West was far less permanent and its effects were more limited than was the case when this same art spread in the countries of the Byzantine missions, and in Sicily and Venice during the preceding period. But this later conquest is perhaps even more astonishing, if one takes into consideration the tremendous flowering of the arts in all the countries of Western Europe during the twelfth and thirteenth centuries. Here we probably have a case of the contributions from outside which an art attracts when in the throes of its own development. Certain of its powers of assimilation, it profits from this contact.

In the artistic geography of Byzantium it is necessary to note several peculiarities, which in some ways are even more important than the frequent overlapping of the territory of the Byzantine state by the area of its artistic expansion.

1. Geographically, Byzantine territory proper is very limited when compared with that of the countries of Western Europe, which created and made regular use of medieval art of Latin origin from the Carolingian to the Gothic age. One must bear this in mind when one compares or contrasts the two traditions, that of the Orthodox East and the Catholic West. Whereas the latter was a collective achievement in which all the great peoples of the Latin world took part, the former was created in Byzantium itself, and was communicated as an established system to the peoples of the Byzantine missionary sphere. Of course these various peoples eventually worked out their particular versions but, except beyond the Danube, they never went beyond the basic rules which define Byzantine art. One must also add another difference which separated the two parallel experiments, those of the Orthodox East and the Catholic West, during the Middle Ages. In the East the experiment only lasted for a relatively short period (and only for a very short time in the countries of the Byzantine mission south of the Danube), because during the fourteenth and fifteenth centuries Byzantium herself and her Balkan clients were influenced in matters of civilization and art by the Muslim conqueror. The period of Turkish rule was to produce nothing in the artistic field — and this pause coincided with the period when the Western countries were only just beginning to experience their extraordinary upsurge.

2. As was the case elsewhere, the different parts of the Byzantine territory were not always equally active in the arts which they practised during the Middle Ages. In the period under review — in other words, in the Iconoclast and Macedonian periods — Byzantium appears not as a traditional country, organically balanced, but as the relic of a much greater whole, which had been made coherent and unified by long centuries of history. The part that remained was soon to organize itself, and to become accustomed to doing without daily contacts with the countries of the Levant, or with the important contributions made by the countries of the eastern Mediterranean, with their rich populations, their wheat and their industries. In this reduced Byzantine state there remained an excess of large cities

around a rather narrow sea, soon to be deprived of its 'hinterland' of Asia Minor. Of these cities only three or four were to remain important, but nevertheless this was enough to make the Byzantine state the only country at that time which counted enough cities of sufficient importance, where the usual activities of an urban population were pursued without interruption from antiquity to the Middle Ages. Crafts of all kinds, including art, had their place and because of this the workshops of Byzantine craftsmen in Constantinople particularly, but also those in Salonika, Smyrna and Corinth were centres where old traditions were maintained and where it was possible to obtain articles of quality. Of course Salonika, Athens and Corinth were devastated by the Arabs and the Normans, but only temporarily, whereas Constantinople remained untouched until 1204. It was this which allowed this great city, and to a lesser degree the other coastal cities of the Aegean Sea, to ensure for centuries the survival of qualified craftsmen, which was a vital necessity for the continuation of art of value. The Byzantine Empire of the Middle Ages was much more favoured from this point of view than the countries of the West, where the Roman cities had nearly all been reduced to large villages. Constantinople was by far the most populous city in all Christendom, even after the rise of the trading ports of Italy — Pisa, Genoa and Venice. Consequently one is not surprised to learn that the main Byzantine works of art were fashioned in Constantinople (the part taken by other cities in this work remains to be established). This was very different from the situation in the West, before the thirteenth century, where the centres of artistic activity were situated not in towns, but in monasteries.

Artistic primacy of Constantinople

The role of certain Byzantine convents was no less important, at least where manuscript-painting was concerned; but the few indications we have from the sources mention mainly the monasteries established in Constantinople itself. These convents of the capital were numerous and well endowed, the most important among them enjoying royal patronage; whether they liked it or not, members of the reigning dynasty and of the great Byzantine families often came to spend the end of their lives there. It would be difficult to differentiate between the art practised within these convents and religious art produced outside their enclosures. Of course in the

Artistic role of certain Byzantine convents

great centres of Byzantine monastic life, such as Mount Athos, all the buildings and all the paintings were done by the monks; it was Denis de Fourna, a monk, who was the author of a post-Byzantine 'Manual of Painting', which has been preserved for us to see. Panselinos, a fourteenth-century painter who enjoyed a great reputation, was an Athonite monk. The frescoes which decorate the

PLATE P. 22

Troglodyte monasteries of Cappadocia are too rustic for us to exclude *a priori* the theory that painters outside the small community of monks were called in. In short, Byzantine monks certainly took part in the execution of religious works of art. But the anonymity of most of these works prevents all evaluation of the relative importance of their participation — and, above all, the style and extent of the works which have been preserved do not allow us to recognize an artistic field limited to monastic workshops.

Difficulty of social classification of Byzantine works

This remark also applies to other social groups. The scarcity of dedicatory inscriptions, and of written information, and also the absence of sufficient differentiation between works of art, prevent any attempt to distinguish between a court art and an art particular to middle-class town dwellers or the like, and attempts made in this direction by various art critics have never led anywhere. Finally, almost no success has been registered in the efforts to distinguish between local or regional schools and workshops. It is of course quite usual to find in various current works assertions to the contrary, and to read that a certain Byzantine work is 'aristocratic' or 'popular', or that it represents the style of Asia Minor rather than that of another province. But when one looks into the question carefully, one finds that these are more or less gratuitous statements. Thus works of quality are generally attributed to the capital, and rustic works are considered to be provincial; works which bear a strong classical influence are said to be of aristocratic and not of monastic origin. Manuscripts with purple sheets are recognized as coming from Constantinople, because purple was the imperial colour. Paintings and sculptures which seem to reflect an Asiatic influence are said to have originated in the eastern provinces of the empire. Now it is quite obvious that these conclusions are valueless and that to each of these apparent theories just as many others can be opposed. However, these uncertainties are in themselves of obvious interest.

They stem from the fact that in our present state of knowledge we are generally unable to establish a connection between the works of art which have been preserved and the geography and social structure of Byzantium. This may be pursued with more success in the future. But we know enough about the Byzantine art of the Middle Ages not to expect any notable progress in this direction, for several general facts make this difficult: the systematic anonymity of Byzantine works, the extreme dearth of written sources, due to the almost total loss of archives, and finally the insufficient differentiation of the works themselves.

This last point is essential, and one can see here a characteristic of medieval Byzantine art, especially when one compares it to the art of the Middle Ages in the West. This is partly due to the fact that the social structure of Byzantium was more stable but less precise than the feudal society of Latin countries. The ethnic uniformity of the Byzantine state, with its overwhelming predominance of Greeks, could also be contrasted with the national diversity of medieval Europe during the period of Romanesque and Gothic art. Let us remind ourselves from now on (we shall return to this in the chapter devoted to architecture) that political, administrative and judicial continuity were for centuries ensured by the imperial power and that of the Patriarch of Constantinople, and that economically, too, during this period Constantinople was the heart of the whole country. All these factors certainly contributed to give a certain uniformity to Byzantine taste and to the need that may have been felt for art. The work of art — particularly in the field of religious art, which we know best — belonged in Byzantium to the realm of the traditional, regularly repeated on similar occasions, where individual temperament or passing sentiment are hardly reflected. This form of art in no way attempts to tell us about the man who *Distance between* initiated it in these regular conditions. If the artist should of *image and reality* necessity express himself, the margin of his intervention is rather narrow and generally limited to nuances of style. It would also be fruitless to look in these Byzantine works, by analysing the subject of the paintings or bas-reliefs, for references to men and to the world in which they lived. There are no such references, no details taken from life, no indiscretions which might indicate the social class or the geographical origin of their authors. Byzantine images, even those which served as illustrations for chronicles, always kept their distance from reality. It is easier to understand the reason for this when saints or sacred events are represented: the irrational is expressed by establishing a distance between the image and material reality. But secular or profane images are just as slow to reflect reality. They remain brief and vague, and impress one by the very absence of sharpness in the reproduction of beings and objects pertaining to everyday life: they are 'symbols' rather than representations. Here we touch upon an essential characteristic of Byzantine art — one which is in opposition both to Muslim and Western art.

This conception of artistic representation in relation to transitory life and the things which support that life, explains what we were saying earlier on: that Byzantine art is difficult to integrate into the historical and geographical background. It touches lightly on what is accidental, including the fate of the individual and even events which are of interest to society. It had its proper role and went its own way. This is a feature to which we will return later. Very exceptional circumstances (such as the Iconoclast edicts of the emperors of the eighth and ninth centuries) were necessary to change this even temporarily. Other happenings did not affect them, and it shows a certain lack of 'historical sense' to expect Byzantine works to provide direct evidence about the social and economic history of Byzantium in the Middle Ages, or about the reactions of a class or an individual to any given event of history, including even religious history.

Relations between Christian faith and art
The overwhelming majority of Byzantine works of art were created in the service of the Church or the Christian faith. This is the essential fact about them. One is entitled to suppose that, as the Church was the main patron of Byzantine art, important changes either in the content of this faith or in its ritual would have created modifications in ecclesiastical art. This is what did in fact happen during the reign of the Iconoclast emperors. But after the end of official Iconoclasm in 843 the religion of the Byzantines was not modified in any perceptible way, or at any rate not in fields which were reflected in art. This was notably the case with liturgy — that

is to say, all the rites celebrated in the Church. As to the heresies which made repeated appearances in the Byzantium of the Middle Ages, they of course troubled the conscience of the Byzantines — but neither the Paulicians, the Bogomils nor the doctrines of John Italus etc. modified in any way the ritual of Byzantine art. Nor were the Hesychasts of the fourteenth century any more active in this field, although the contrary has several times been maintained, and we may possibly owe them a few iconographic details: e.g. images of the Transfiguration on Mount Tabor, with the idea of distinguishing three lights, symbols of the three persons of the Trinity in the halo surrounding the Risen Christ. Later studies may perhaps increase the number of alterations that the Hesychasts made to iconographic tradition. But in any case they will never be more than details, as there is an obvious continuity in Byzantine traditions before and after the Hesychasts. Similarly, we can dismiss the influence of Catholic art, which did penetrate into Byzantine territory, notably in the thirteenth century. Of course, more or less superficial influences derived from Latin art can be observed here and there during that period and subsequently. But when one remembers the extraordinary flowering of religious art in the West from the eleventh century onwards, the extreme modesty of its influence on Byzantium never ceases to surprise us. It would undoubtedly have been difficult to reflect in art the break with Rome in 1054. But, after all, Catholic art in the sixteenth century reflects the Reformation. This was not the case in Byzantium; at any rate, there is next to nothing in the works of art which have been preserved. They ignore totally the break between the Greek and Latin churches.

In this Christian Byzantine art there are no reflections of either the birth of Islam or the flowering of Islamic art. Here again the example *The Christian art of Byzantium and Islam* of the West, so receptive to Muslim creations in architecture and interior decoration, only makes us even more aware of the extreme reserve of the Byzantines. One might have thought that it was a deliberately negative attitude; but it is more a general refusal, probably a tacit one, to allow themselves to be influenced by the events which affected contemporary religious life. As we shall see, it was on a different level that certain Muslim contributions to Byzantine art took place, and they appear only in ornamental decoration or at the most in certain manuscripts, particularly secular ones.

When all is said, one must admit that the religious art of the Byzantines, superbly indifferent to things of the world, was little influenced by the fluctuations of the history of religious life itself. That does not in any way mean that those who practised this art daily were not themselves passionately interested in all that concerned the faith and administration of the Church. In Constantinople people perhaps suffered rather from an excess of interest in theology, and there were many famous discussions on matters of faith. But figurative Byzantine art was not concerned in this, and this fact, although a negative one, is characteristic.

So we are concerned with a form of art which was an independent activity within Byzantine civilization, and which did not react at all to political, social and ecclesiastical events; nor did communities or individuals expect to find their particular experiences reflected in it. We are dealing with a form of activity inherited by medieval Byzantium from an earlier period, with its procedures, its techniques and its tastes, which the Greeks of that period continued without perceptibly modifying its formulas. Later we shall give the positive characteristics of Byzantine works of art, only pointing out in this outline that the historic and geographical background was a very stable one during the period we are studying, because of the nature of Byzantine art and the limited number of factors capable of giving it stimulus. However, to make things easier, we shall distinguish in this work between the four traditional periods:

THE FOUR TRADITIONAL PERIODS

The Iconoclast Period
The Reign of the Macedonians
The Reign of the Comneni
The Reign of the Palaeologi.

The very titles of these periods, called after the dynasties, underline the artificial character of this division, but in so far as essentials go, artistic life went on without apparent changes from the end of Iconoclasm up to the fall of Constantinople, and each of these periods possesses features which are its alone. These particularities are not necessarily linked to political, social or other events, and they are not even exclusive to this or that period, but each period had its own way of accenting tradition; or at any rate, this is what is suggested by the essential works of each of these successive periods. The Iconoclast period attempted a form of art without figurative images — a Christian version of aniconical religious art, such as was at the same time inaugurated by the Muslims.

The emperors of the Macedonian dynasty attempted to create around themselves a *renovatio* of the arts and the literature of antiquity. So far as art is concerned we only know what effect it had on religious works. These magnificently proclaim achievements of Greek taste in the arts, but they also prove the limitations of this renaissance. This period corresponds to a general burst of activity in Byzantium, where works of art of different tendencies flowered at the same time. The antique tendency was undoubtedly the most remarkable, but the particular Byzantine style of the Middle Ages evolved during this period, which more than any other in the history of Byzantium deserves the title of the 'golden age'.

It is obvious that the limits which separate these periods are not strict ones. It is in consequence practical to start the third period only in the last third of the eleventh century, with the advent of the first Comnenus, and to prolong it up to 1204. The greatest number of Byzantine or Byzantine-inspired monuments, churches, mosaics, frescoes, miniatures, ivories and ceramics belong to the eleventh and twelfth centuries. They are of a well-established style which codified the creations of the preceding period. But it was also under the Comneni that the aesthetics of centuries to come were evolved and future tendencies suggested.

During the fifty years of the Latin Empire of Constantinople Byzantine works are almost entirely non-existent. But the works of the twelfth century prepare the way for those which appeared at the end of the thirteenth, after the restoration of the Greek Empire. In architecture and particularly in painting this was to be another and final *renovatio* which, parallel with the art of the Italian Dugento and Quattrocento and of the new creations of the northern European countries, attempted to recast inherited traditions into a form of art, at the same time faithful to established usages and yet rather different — and probably better adapted to the demands of a more advanced age.

There is always something to be gained from limiting artistic activity to a given sphere. To define it is to add to our knowledge of this art. In Byzantium during the Middle Ages much the same work was done as during the epoch which preceded the Iconoclast period — i.e., the time of Justinian and his immediate successors. This does not, however, mean that artistic activity was pursued with the same intensity everywhere and at all times. The means which a Justinian had at his disposal were no longer available to his successors in the Middle Ages, and for various reasons certain aspects of traditional art were suspended or abandoned, whereas others took on increased importance.

THE ICONOCLAST PERIOD

Thus during the Iconoclast period one whole field, the representation of religious figures, was suddenly abandoned. But secular painting and all aspects of decorative art, iconical and aniconical, were able to continue — and there is nothing to prevent us from thinking that there was any decrease in the volume of artistic activity in this field. It has often been thought that the abandoning of iconographic representation must have favoured the sector of secular and decorative art which was called upon to replace it. Unfortunately the works of this period were systematically destroyed later and the texts which speak about them were written by enemies of the Iconoclasts. This falsifies our information on the subject. In any case, it would appear that the Iconoclast period, above all a time of incessant wars which ravaged the country and exhausted its economic potential, was poor in artistic achievements. However, churches were certainly built everywhere, during this period as before and after, and at the extreme end of the Iconoclast period the Emperor Theophilus took an active part in renewing the splendours of his great palace in Constantinople. The success of the imperial armies allowed this expenditure, and the prestige of the sovereign in the eyes of the Carolingians and the caliphs justified it.

All these monuments have disappeared without leaving any trace — and more particularly the written sources, which alone gave information on art under the Iconoclasts, mention only a few isolated monuments. It is impossible, knowing as little as we do, to reconstitute the extent of the artistic activities of this period.

The Orthodox victory of 843 changed everything — and there are several reasons for this. On the one hand this period is represented by numerous monuments which still remain, and on the other the political and economic growth from the end of the ninth to the end of the eleventh century favoured the erection of sumptuous buildings and encouraged orders for movable works of all kinds. There was intense artistic activity in Byzantium and we are in a good position to imagine its scope and its programme. ART AFTER THE ORTHODOX VICTORY

Architecture is mainly represented by religious buildings. Again a fair number of them were built in the capital and in the provinces. The example was set by the emperors, who were emulated by state dignitaries and members of the great families. A characteristic aspect of this art was the restoration and reconstruction by the emperors of Justinian's sanctuaries and other old buildings. They looked back, showing themselves to be less creators than guardians of a tradition to be maintained. ARCHITECTURE

Another tradition which they wished to keep up is illustrated by the works of Justinian and other patrons of the last centuries of antiquity — the tradition of luxurious and expensive interior decoration of all 'houses of God', which were made as rich as the emperor's palace. Basil I, the Macedonian, gave the example, or rather revived that of his distant predecessors. He was himself constantly imitated during the tenth, eleventh and twelfth centuries by sovereigns such as Romanus Lecapenus, Constantine IX Monomachus, and Manuel and John Comnenus. Less wealthy, the Palaeologi did their best to remain faithful to the traditional patronage of the *basileis*, benefactors of the shrines of the capital and at times even of those of the provinces. There are still in existence, here and there, and especially in St. Mark's in Venice, the gifts of the Byzantine sovereigns to the churches of Constantinople — chalices, patens, reliquaries, lamps, votive crowns, bound Gospels, all in gold or silver gilt, studded with cabochons, pearls and enamels. The most beautiful pieces, which are also the richest and the most numerous, date back to the tenth and eleventh centuries; works less perfect, but still of fairly good quality, belong to the twelfth century; and there are still some

Religious buildings. The richness of their interior decoration

PLATE P. 68

valuable ones which belong to the fourteenth and even the fifteenth centuries. In other words, during the whole of the Middle Ages churches continued to be built and to be provided with liturgical vessels, embroideries, icons and books — the latter often illustrated and encased in artistic bindings. This constitutes the central, as well as the richest category of Byzantine art in the Middle Ages.

PLATES PP. 19, 67

PLATES PP. 40, 63, 66, 70, 87

These same churches were regularly panelled with mosaics, or even more often with mural paintings. Every church and every chapel presents a remarkable ensemble of religious figuration, the figures forming a cycle conceived and articulated according to an erudite system. Other cycles of painting decorate religious books, beginning with the Gospels. A few of these illuminated and richly decorated manuscripts complete the series of objects which were indispensable to the liturgical cult. But others were destined for convent libraries where sermon writers, hagiographers and theologians consulted them in order to fulfil better their clerical duties and to improve their religious knowledge.

PLATES PP. 43, 46

OBJECTS OF WORSHIP

Through certain of these illustrated books of a more popular nature we get closer to works of art which correspond to those which people wished to have for private worship: icons of every type, of different sizes, in different materials, and made by different techniques, as well as pectoral crosses and medallions which replaced the traditional amulets. We know of a mass of objects of this type in which one finds great art as well as the product of a modest industry designed for the use of pilgrims — all of which, however, belongs to the realm of religious art. Throughout the Middle Ages Byzantium never ceased its enormous production in this field. In order to appreciate the volume of this industry on several different levels, and also the reputation which these objects enjoyed, one need only go over the lists of reliquaries, icons and crosses which the crusaders of the Fourth Crusade sent from Constantinople to their native countries: the *exuviae sacrae* of Constantinople in 1204 would fill a museum. When one considers the various categories of Byzantine religious monuments, one has the strong impression that one is dealing with a complex and coherent whole, of which one knows all the important aspects. If there was a field in which the Byzantines demanded the participation of art at all times, in all its forms, and made use of all

Techniques and materials of religious art

its techniques, it was the religious field. Every aspect of worship and piety was served by one or more artistic techniques, at every artistic level, from the great artist's masterpiece to the crude attempts of the village artisan. In this field the city of Byzantium was distinctly privileged, since it preserved every technique of craftsmanship and all the materials, including the rarest and the most valuable. This means of course that from antiquity onwards there was uninterrupted activity in the various workshops of the specialized craftsmen: stone-masons, carpenters, cutters of both ordinary and semi-precious stones (porphyry, marble, malachite, onyx, serpentine, etc.), glass-blowers, enamellers, goldsmiths, mosaicists, fresco-painters, miniaturists, saddlers, workers in ivory, etc. There is even a special field, that of cloisonné enamel work with figures, which seems to have been perfected in Byzantium at the beginning of the period we are studying. This gave birth to a new art industry of which wide use was made for the decoration of ecclesiastical objects. PLATES PP. 44, 45

Compared with religious art, secular art seems poor — fewer works of art, less scope for these works, less technical variety, and a noticeable recession when compared to the earliest Byzantine period — when, however, the role played by secular art was more important than at any other time during the Middle Ages. SECULAR ART

As is often the case, Byzantine secular architecture and particularly the dwellings of the Middle Ages have practically all disappeared. There is only one such building of artistic interest which is still standing in Constantinople, the ruined palace known as Tekfur-Serai, from the fourteenth century. The most important imperial palaces have all been destroyed. But we know that many buildings were continually put up and that they were rich, built in various styles, with domes up to the middle of the twelfth century, at least, and again in the fourteenth. Even if the architecture of Byzantine palaces mainly eludes us, we can be certain that they knew how to build them on a considerable scale and with richly decorated interiors. Texts speak of mosaics and mural paintings on secular subjects, which decorated these palaces of the Middle Ages — and, in the mosaics of the Royal Palace in Palermo, their echo has been preserved. ARCHITECTURE

Palaces

APPX. PL. 14

PLATE P. 39

Apart from this, of the secular minor arts we only possess a few fragments of beautiful illuminated silk materials, vases in crystal and moulded glass, in semi-precious stone, small ivories, diadems, enamel and niello bracelets. In addition to all this, which belonged to the special field of feminine adornment, there were three other sectors in which secular art registered a steady activity in the Middle Ages. In the first place there was the art devoted to the emperor and the glorification of his power. It is represented during this period only by portraits of the *basileus* and *basilissa*, by scenes of their coronation, or by numerous ornamental decorations in the manuscripts, where in the margins of religious texts images already known in antiquity were represented, but on a larger scale. Then again there were illustrations in medical books, hunting works and chronicles — another heritage of antiquity kept in a fossilized state in a small number of works which were copied and re-copied because these explanatory paintings continued to fulfil their original role with the readers. In other words, the field of Byzantine secular art during the Middle Ages was infinitely more restricted than that of religious art.

Art devoted to the emperor

PLATE P. 20

Illustrations in scientific books and chronicles

When trying to define the respective fields of various arts in Byzantium, one must take into account certain fluctuations. It was during the tenth and eleventh centuries that artistic activities were most varied. Flourishing in Constantinople, but in Corinth and Thessalonica as well, the arts and crafts then also included luxury techniques such as the weaving of silks with figurative decorations, small sculptures in ivory and precious metals (solid and embossed surfaces), glyptics, the cutting of semi-precious stones, artistic glassware, glazed potteries, niello and cloisonné enamelware, the glory of Byzantium. It is established that certain of these art techniques remained in use during the twelfth century; during the Comnenian period there were small pieces of ivory sculpture, enamels and embossed silver and gold ware. But the pieces which date from this more advanced period are rarer and often of inferior quality. These objects were widely produced, and several of the techniques we have mentioned were no longer in use after the eleventh century.

Artistic crafts from Xth to XIIth century

One gains the impression that in order to maintain the splendour of their art the Byzantines of the twelfth century limited its variety, and that — apart from traditional monumental art (including of course frescoes and mural mosaics) — they concentrated on pieces of sculpture, with a predominance of embossed surfaces worked with very thin sheets of silver, and on top of enamel decorations. On the other hand the increased output of works of this type was not achieved without endangering their quality. In other words, well before the sack of Constantinople by the Crusaders in 1204 there occurred a decline in the luxury arts of the Byzantines. We cannot say anything more precise as to the stages of this decline, which may have taken place following the development of similar activities in all the neighbouring countries — in Latin Europe as well as in the countries of the Byzantine mission, in the Caucasus, in the Balkans and in Russia. This emancipation from Byzantium may have resulted in a decrease in corresponding works in Byzantium itself.

Small sculpture in the XIIth century

This decline was final so far as the spread of artistic activities was concerned. Although Byzantine art experienced a new impetus after the reconquest of Constantinople in 1261, it never succeeded in attaining the greatness of the tenth and eleventh centuries. Original architecture concerned itself practically only with churches. Monumental painting (frescoes and mosaics) — reserved for churches only (?) — maintained its traditional function, as did icons (movable religious paintings, generally on wood). Other painting techniques — pictures in manuscripts, paintings with coloured enamels — became much rarer and were hardly ever excellent. Glyptics, carved semi-precious stones, and sculptures on ivory were in total decadence. Pottery and artistic glass remained on a very modest level.

BYZANTINE ART AFTER THE RECONQUEST OF CONSTANTINOPLE

Only the flowering of embroidery dates from the Palaeologian period. At a time when every branch of Byzantine art was on the decline everywhere, artistic embroidery alone conquered new territory. This form of art remained in favour with all the heirs of Byzantium after the fall of the empire in 1453. The only examples of this embroidery we know of were those in ecclesiastical use.

We must finally note an important negative fact: monumental sculpture played an insignificant part in Byzantine art during the

BYZANTINE SCULPTURE IN THE MIDDLE AGES

37

Middle Ages. Contrary to what has sometimes been said, the Byzantine Church never pronounced itself against statuary and it is certainly not to any official order that one can attribute the absence during the Middle Ages of any plastic figuration work of importance. It is interesting to remember that Byzantium continued to practise a certain form of statuary — sculpted effigies of emperors — far longer than did the West, in fact up to about 800. It was probably the Iconoclast movement begun in 726 which was fatal to Byzantine statuary; for after the rebirth of figurative images in 843, statuary had no place, and the only form of plastic art which continued were bas-reliefs with small-scale figures and purely decorative sculpture.

Nevertheless sufficient justice has not been rendered to the work of Byzantine sculptors of the Middle Ages. Modest as their work was, it deserves a better place, and in particular it should be studied in connection with the origins of Romanesque sculpture. One must, however, admit that, compared with medieval art in Western Europe, the absence of monumental sculpture and the infrequent use of architectural sculpture certainly count among the major characteristics (negative though they are) of Byzantine medieval art. This absence is all the more surprising, of course, as we are dealing with the art of those same Greeks who several centuries earlier were sculptors first and foremost.

PLATE 5 – Trees and hunting scene. Mosaic in 'Roger's Chamber' in the Royal Palace, Palermo, *ca.* 1160. *Cf. p. 35*

PLATE 6 – Two saints. Mosaic at Hosios Lucas in Phocis, *ca.* 1000. *Cf. p. 34*

PLATE 7 – Victory of Constantine on the Milvius Bridge before Rome. Miniature, ca. 885. *Bibliothèque Nationale, Paris (MS. Grec 510). Cf. p. 170*

PLATE 8 – A personage walking in the woods. xıth-century miniature, in a work on snake-bites by Nicander. *Bibliothèque Nationale, Paris (MS. Grec Suppl. 247). Cf. p. 168*

PLATE 9 – Decorative painting on a page of the Canons of the Gospels, xith century. *Bibliothèque Nationale, Paris (MS. Grec 64). Cf. pp. 34, 179, 181.*

43

PLATE 10 – A vase in red and black glass bearing mythological subjects painted with enamel, xɪth century. *Treasury of St. Mark's, Venice. Cf. p. 35*

PLATE II – Christ on a Byzantine intaglio, xth-xith century. *Cabinet des Médailles, Paris. Cf. p. 35*

PLATE 12 – St. John the Evangelist. Miniature in a book of Gospels, xivth century. *Cf. pp. 34, 179*

III. TECHNIQUES

Most of the techniques which the Byzantines employed during the Middle Ages were the same as those in use all over the Mediterranean. They nearly all date back to antiquity. This heritage, common to all of the Greek and Latin world, was adopted in a different way by each people, and their choice varied.

The Eastern Empire managed to survive the invasions which ravaged the Western world and, thanks to this, Constantinople was able to pursue without interruption the normal activities of a great Mediterranean city. More of the techniques of art and the luxury trades were preserved here than elsewhere, and this contributed to the reputation which the Byzantine capital enjoyed in the eyes of its neighbours in Europe and Asia. This prestige can be measured by the calls made on Byzantine mosaicists by Damascus and Cordova, by the imitation of their miniatures in Germany and even England, and by the acquisition of Byzantine works in gold, silver and enamel by all the countries of the Christian world. In the eleventh century a monk with the Greek-sounding name of Theodore published in the Rhineland a *Schedula diversarum artium* or compendium of technical recipes relating to the various arts, in which a great number of the recipes for luxury glass, gold and silverware were attributed to the Greeks. What knowledge we have from the Byzantine works which have been preserved, prove the high technical quality.

Prestige of Constantinople in techniques of art and luxury trades

The Byzantines built a great deal during the Middle Ages, but neither the architectural planners of the period nor the masons or stone-carvers who executed their plans seem to have possessed much technical knowledge. Byzantine architecture of that period made use of brick and did so quite well, but the Persian masons who built the Iranian monuments of that period (Muslim religious architecture) were far more skilled in the use of baked bricks for building and decoration. The Byzantine buildings also compare unfavourably with the monuments in rough or carved stone, built by their Western, Muslim and Transcaucasian contemporaries.

ARCHITECTURE

PAINTING As soon as we enter the field of painting the picture alters. Byzantine mural mosaics are incomparably superior to similar works executed elsewhere. During the Middle Ages portable mosaic works did not exist outside Byzantium. As for mural paintings proper, the Byzantines had no monopoly, but the frescoes executed by Greek artists, at any rate up to the twelfth century, are by far the most skilful and the most beautiful. The same can also be said of their manuscript paintings, which were often not only beautiful but also the most faithful guardians of antique traditions of painting.

The technical superiority of all categories of Byzantine paintings has been recognized in Western Europe and the Near East by both *Mosaics* Christians and Muslims. There are indeed very few mosaics to be found anywhere that are not either the work of Greek artists or imitations of Byzantine models. The quality of these mosaics improved steadily to the extent that the Byzantines took part in their creation. If portable mosaics were not made outside Byzantium, it was surely due to the difficulty of handling the microscopic cubes of which they are composed.

Close study reveals the skill involved in a technique which makes the impact of an image depend simultaneously on the colour, shape and size of each small coloured cube. On their grouping, on the uneven spaces which separated them, and on the slant of each cube in relation to the wall depend the intensity and the quality of the light which they reflect. It is through observing mural paintings of the twelfth and thirteenth centuries in Italy, Germany, Spain and elsewhere in the West, and by comparing them to older frescoes in these same countries, that one can best understand what Romanesque artists learned in the field of technique from Greek artists and their works. They taught them the use of a certain scale of colours in which warm and bright shades predominated (reds, browns, cobalt and dark blues), and showed them how, by making use of these colours, one could model bodies and draperies with far greater suppleness than the Romanesque painters had done in the past.

Painting It was in manuscript paintings that the Byzantine artists remained *in manuscripts* most faithful to the technical precepts of the ancients, either by repeating the same pictures step by step, or by purposely falling back on much older models. As material conditions (parchment,

48

colours, fixatives) had not altered, these small pictures were produced in the same way at the end of antiquity as they were during the Middle Ages: the parchment was prepared in the same way (a fine coating of plaster was spread beneath the colours), and the same scale and method were used to represent the head, eyes, garment folds, light and shade. In the case of miniatures, too, one may grasp the superiority of Byzantine techniques over others by comparing the paintings in the Latin, Armenian and Syrian manuscripts which were influenced by them with those which were not. Apart from these contributions of style, the Byzantines gave their miniatures a deeper and richer scale of colours, and above all passed on that major heritage of Greek tradition: the art of modelling the human body and draperies.

But it was in the technique of the luxury trades that they especially LUXURY TRADES excelled, having inherited, as we have said, more than one traditional technique of antiquity and having perfected certain arts themselves: they were also submitted to the influence of the arts of Asia. Gold and silver work, decorated with polychrome cabochons, was executed with great success in Byzantium, although it is not possible to single out specifically the Byzantine versions in the examples where this type of decoration was applied. On the other hand the filigree threads which sometimes line Byzantine works of gold and silver during the Middle Ages are the finest which exist, and they are of a peculiar type. Byzantine filigree work is recognizable by the *Filigree* way the gold threads are plaited and adapted to the ornamental motifs and to the object which they decorate, and also to the pearls, cabochons and enamels which surround them. The filigree pieces of the Ottonian gold- and silversmiths are the most closely related, as they were influenced by Byzantine models.

At the present time we know little of the technique of the Byzantine *Incrustations of one* gold- and silversmiths, which consisted of incrusting one metal into *metal into another* the other, and particularly of fixing strips of gold and silver into silver and bronze to form ornaments, or even human beings and scenes. The best-known examples of this technique are the doors of churches preserved in Italy, which were sent there from Constantinople. The Italian imitations of this work, however good they may be, do not come up to the standard of those made by Byzantine craftsmen. On these doors, on various ritual objects and particularly on the bindings of liturgical Gospels, as well as on the frames of venerated icons we find these sheaths of silver and gold leaf, chased in relief on moulds, representing ornaments, personages and scenes. Raised work of this kind sometimes occupied the main panel of an icon and gave the impression of relief on solid metal. This technique was more typical of Byzantium than the other we have mentioned, but apparently it made mass production possible and was cheaper. It was easily imitated in Italy and in the other countries of Byzantine influence.

Pre-eminence of enamel cloisonné on gold

However, of all the pottery it was enamel cloisonné on gold which was the greatest of the Byzantine artistic techniques, and it allowed them to create very beautiful works. From the Middle Ages on they were very much sought after in Western Europe. These Byzantine enamels are called 'cloisonné' because tiny gold partitions separate the colours. It was into these partitions that coloured powders were poured, which heat then transformed into poly-chrome paste. The depth of the layer of enamel, which is semi-transparent, and the final polish of the surface, which should be even, are both essential. The immediate origins of this enamel work as it was done in the workshops of Constantinople and by those who imitated it elsewhere, have not been established because of a total lack of detailed studies on the subject, and also perhaps because so few of the works are dated. Certain of the oldest pieces use cloisonné enamel side by side with ground-moulded glass enclosed in the partitions. This suggests the following hypothesis: enamel may have replaced incrustations of multi-coloured stones and polychrome glass. It was probably not earlier than the beginning of the period which we are examining in this book, i.e. the ninth century, that the technique of working enamel was perfected (for example, a means of obtaining a richer scale of colour whose shades could be predicted) so as to allow it to go beyond its traditional field, that of ornamental decor, into the representation of figures, which was really a kind of painting. Byzantine enamel of the Middle Ages made use of the techniques of painting and in this respect can be compared to mosaics: to portable mosaics particularly, as enamel colours were difficult to apply to large surfaces, unless the separate pieces were assembled side by side. This work can also be compared to the stained glass of the West. The glowing colours obtained with the help of enamels were as good as and even better than those in mosaics. Attempts to imitate it were made, and its influences as well as that of gold and silver work can be found in the painted decoration of Byzantine manuscripts. This same influence on local miniaturists was also exercised by Limoges enamels. The enameller's art flourished as much there as in Byzantium, but use was made of a different technique (*champlevé*).

The Byzantines knew about this different method of fixing colours on metal, which consisted of lightly hollowing out the surface (hence the term *champlevé*) and then filling in these cavities with enamel. But this cruder method was employed only for ornamentation and for small objects in solid metal. The cavities were larger and in consequence the colours were more clearly separated from each other and more opaque. At this level — in the case of rings, for example — closely related colours are less numerous, and the enamelling was hardly distinguishable from the technique of niello. Niello ornaments, including reproductions of figures on small objects, were also among the gold and silver works produced in the Byzantine workshops. Silver objects in particular were decorated in this way, the result being a cheaper form of enamel ware. *Champlevé method*

It is generally felt that luxury arts developed in Byzantium in the shadow of the imperial court. However plausible this may be, since the court was of course one of the principal patrons of the craftsmen who made these objects, there are no literary texts or inscriptions which establish the existence of courtly mosaic or silver- and goldsmiths' workshops. On the other hand inscriptions on illuminated textiles which have been preserved (ninth–eleventh centuries) prove the existence of workshops where precious silks were woven. Certain of them were located at the gates of the great imperial palace (the Zeuxippe workshops), while others were situated elsewhere, even far away (Corinth) although they worked for the emperor. He possessed the monopoly of the production and the sale of certain luxury materials and his officials dealt severely with frauds. It appears that these workshops existed from the earliest period of Byzantine history. This is borne out by an in- *Precious illuminated textiles* scription on a textile which may be attributed to Heraclea on the Propontis in the fourth century. Nevertheless the decor of textiles coming from the imperial workshops of the ninth–eleventh centuries was in great part of Iranian inspiration, Sassanid or post-Sassanid. For examples of these see the animals on silk of Saint-Josse, Pas-de-Calais, in the Louvre, which an inscription allows us to attribute to the tenth century and to an eastern province of Persia. In fact the art industry of which the emperors owned the monopoly encouraged and spread an Oriental, rather than a truly Byzantine form of art. Active as privileged traders, the emperors made use of what was produced by the highly qualified technicians in their service.

This summary of the artistic techniques on which medieval Byzantine art was based is intended to prove this major fact: that one of the main qualities of Byzantine work is due to the presence of technicians who knew the secrets of several reputedly difficult artistic crafts which were not something that could be improvised. The high proportion of work of extremely fine quality is a proof of this. Less now than in the past, too much emphasis has been laid on the usual disadvantages this could bring about, i.e. the weight of routine which could stifle creative instinct. There is no doubt that routine was extremely powerful in the workshops of Byzantine mosaicists, glass-blowers, carvers of precious stones, silver- and goldsmiths and weavers. The counterpart of this was no less important — that is to say, the precision, finish and refinement of shapes and colours, the knowledge of proportions, the sureness of their taste, the experience of generations of highly select craftsmen — all these reduced the risk of accidental mistakes being made by an individual. One of the reasons why Byzantine art in the Middle Ages was never vulgar is due to the prestige of this tradition, which here more than elsewhere, and for obvious reasons, was maintained in the work produced by artisans who specialized in different techniques. These same techniques, because of their scarcity and the expense of the materials of which they made use, revealed new aesthetic values in the relationships between shapes, materials and colours. The extreme distinction of Byzantine works was in great part due to these aesthetic refinements carried out by craftsmen who were trained in the workshops of the same cities for many generations.

Byzantine art owes a great deal to the skilful techniques employed in the creation of these works, by which is meant both the quality of the material production and the influence these techniques wielded over their aesthetic expression.

IV. THE INFLUENCE OF IDEAS

As everywhere and always, the art that flourished in Byzantium owed a great deal to the ideas which circulated there. But of these ideas — the result of intellectual approaches and of the feelings of individuals or groups of various sizes — it appears that only very few had any effect on artistic life. It is to these few ideas that the following pages will be devoted. We must, however, warn our readers that we will merely mention some aspects of this problem, as the destruction of a great number of monuments prevents us at present from taking these into consideration, despite the very real influence which they may have had.

Influence of Byzantine monarchical thought on art

As soon as we start considering the ideological background of Byzantine art in the Middle Ages, we immediately realize the gaps in our information. One has only to remember that the Byzantines lived under the rule of a monarchy of divine right, strongly influenced by a theocratic doctrine; Constantine and the proponents of Christian theocracy created an empire governed by a lieutenant of Christ on earth, and thereafter this conception of the Byzantine state was never abandoned. This did not mean, at least in theory, that the Church too was governed by the emperor. The Byzantine church found its spiritual sources directly in God, without having to go through the monarch — the lieutenant of God. The respective powers of the Church and the sovereign stemmed from the same source, but in a parallel fashion. This doctrine was difficult to apply to political life, as it was generally the stronger of the two who prevailed, that is to say the monarch. Without insisting on the mere fact of an autocratic government and the importance of imperial influence in every field, one can imagine *a priori* that Byzantine art reflected monarchical thought. The theory and practice of imperial power in general and its concrete acts should have found expression in art, all the more so because the immediate antecedents in the ancient Roman Empire favoured the development of an imperial Byzantine art of this type. The elements of such an art, which are reflections of political doctrines based on the monarchy with its theories and practical activities, do indeed exist and bear witness to the influence of these ideas. One sees at any rate that certain figurative art with symbolic tendencies was meant to express through images the power of the monarch, the divine origin of this power, the duties of the prince and his subjects and the successful role he played. Unfortunately the mass destruction of secular works, beginning with the palaces, limits our field of study. The disappearance of the Great Palace of Constantinople with its mosaics and its paintings and all the insignia of the power of the emperors, and the lack even of faithful reproductions of all these objects, apart from a few typological portraits, deprive us of a great deal of potential evidence on the contribution which political ideas made to Byzantine artistic works.

Even less remains of the works of art which the great families of the Byzantine landed aristocracy commissioned for themselves. From the twelfth century onwards these families played an essential role in the political life of the Byzantine state. Owing to the lack of monuments and to the insufficient number of secular works which the aristocracy called into being we are not in a position to discuss their importance. The only way in which we can gain some impression of them is to study the artistic monuments founded by imperial patrons who came from these families, or those erected by princes who governed in countries under Byzantine influence. Apart from the most important, who tried to imitate imperial patronage, the majority of them followed the example of members of the great aristocratic families. There are many works of this origin dating from the thirteenth and fourteenth centuries. But as we shall see, during this period the princely foundations were mainly sanctuaries, and if one excluded the donor's portrait, it was merely in the choice and interpretation of religious art that the influence of the patron was able to exercise itself.

Role of aristocratic and princely patrons

What is certain, on the other hand, is the idea that these patrons had of the religious usefulness (and perhaps also social usefulness, i.e. the patron's prestige) of their initiatives, which could only have been taken within the framework of the Byzantine Orthodox state. A proof of this is the extreme rarity and at times the total cessation

IMPORTANCE
OF RELIGIOUS
CONCEPTS
IN ART

of undertakings of this kind under either Turkish domination or Latin rule. It was in fact a question of political power, and there is no better proof of the negative influence of ideas — in the form of a complete halt of any artistic activity — than the action of the Iconoclast emperors.

The period treated in this work starts precisely in this era, when for more than a century a religious idea proclaimed by the emperors prevented their Christian subjects from fashioning images. Inversely, there were other ideas related to the value of religious images which later gave a new start to Byzantine figurative painting and sculpture. Later on we shall see that this influence of iconoclast and iconophile ideas was not limited to forbidding or allowing artistic figurative images of God and the Saints. It is not abstract iconoclasm that we have to deal with in Byzantium in the eighth and ninth centuries, but a series of ideas which, rejecting religious imagery, favoured certain others, monarchic ones for example, but only certain ones of this kind. What this means is that, in a series of ideas which may appear as a whole, certain of them are reflected in art, whereas others are not, because they come up against stronger contrary influences, or perhaps because the world into which they penetrated was not yet attuned to such an aspect of thought. Thus the iconoclast doctrine of the emperors of the eighth and ninth centuries might also have made them give up effigies of themselves; whereas in fact they did not do so, but even introduced into the imagery of their coins groups of imperial portraits, featuring not only the reigning monarch but also several of his ancestors. They separated the fields of religious and political imagery and paid particular attention to the interests of the dynasty. It was the dynastic idea which won the day when the Iconoclast emperors had to decide how art was to be applied to their monetary images.

RELIGIOUS FUNCTION OF PRACTICALLY ALL BYZANTINE WORKS OF ART

Ideas connected with religion came to influence Byzantine medieval art on a far wider scale and with a great variety of possible applications which were often realized in practice. It is a general and universally recognized fact that the immense majority of Byzantine works of art had a religious function. In architecture, churches and other religious buildings predominate. All the mosaics and frescoes, and the majority of miniatures, as well as movable sculptured and painted works, deal with Christian subjects and were used for Christian worship. In this art religious ideas, as understood in Byzantium in the Middle Ages, reigned supreme.

However, when attempting to be precise one realizes that certain Christian ideas played a vital part, whereas others did not find their way into art. As to the latter, one is surprised to find that neither the temporary schism of the period of Patriarch Photius at the end of the ninth century, nor the final breach with Rome in 1054 find the slightest reflection in the arts of Byzantium. One can say that no attempt was made to show this separation or to insist on Greek Orthodoxy in pictures. Later, in the thirteenth and fourteenth centuries, when Latin Catholics and Greek Orthodox confronted each other everywhere and an acute struggle developed between clerics and even laymen, their controversies never seem to have touched upon art, or at least upon iconography and the arrangement of churches. As far as I know, there exists no illustrated treatment of the Greek polemics against the Latins, nor was any mural painting in a Greek Orthodox church ever transformed into an image of anti-Roman propaganda. One is led to think that religious Byzantine art was on a level which avoided this type of controversy. Another negative finding which seems to us to suggest one of the most profound characteristics of Byzantine art is its lack of specialization. Whether one is dealing with the churches themselves or the images which decorated them, with their contents or their interior arrangement, one finds that architectural forms and iconographic schemes seem to have no distinct characteristics when applied to cathedrals, monastic or parish churches, or even to private mortuary chapels. The absence of specificity as to the function of the place of worship was of course not absolute, and the churches of the great monasteries do show some functional peculiarities (large narthex, lateral apse). However, these differences are minimal when compared with the characteristics with which Western medieval art endows every category of church, every essential part of the religious building, each iconographic whole that was grafted on to these places of worship. There was of course some change in the interpretation of the architecture of a typical church in the Byzantine world between the end of antiquity and the Middle Ages. But apart

Byzantine sacred art above certain religious controversies

Absence of specificity in the architecture or decoration of places of worship

from the style of architecture and figurative works, which did alter more than once during the Middle Ages, architects, artists and decorators do not seem to have attempted to modify the schemes or the forms which they inherited from their predecessors, but to have concentrated instead on the quality of their reproductions. Their role can be compared to that of musical performers in our day, who do not feel that their importance is diminished by the fact that they limit their talent to the interpretation of other people's works, since each interpretation contains original nuances.

The Byzantine painters of the Middle Ages and of later periods have often been criticized for this attitude. On the one hand this criticism can also be applied to Byzantine religious architecture, and to the schemes of mural paintings in these churches, as well as to other types of Byzantine works. But on the other hand this method should not be considered as a form of poverty. The comparison with the musical performer, often celebrated for his virtuosity, sensitivity and taste, allows us to make our point and to understand better the nature of the Byzantine monuments we are examining. They are nearly always replicas of other very similar works. This applies equally to architecture, mosaics, miniatures, ivory carvings, etc. But each replica is an original work, because in the Middle Ages the reproduction of a motif or an image never meant slavish copying. What was reproduced was the backcloth which in fact has very little to do with the essence of the artistic work. We realize this much better today than before the advent of photography. It is in connection with what are called 'abstracts' — that is to say, works which do not attempt to imitate the appearance of either a person or an object — that we often hear the following remark made: artistic creativity is shown not in the imitation of a model, whether from nature or from a work of art, but through the sensitivity which the artist expresses on this occasion, through plastic, pictorial or architectural means. Precisely this formula best describes the part played by the Byzantine artist who undertook to create a church, a mosaic or an ivory sculpture. If one takes the trouble to look carefully at each of these works one will see the artist's aesthetic originality. Nevertheless, whatever the talent or the personality of the artist may have been, his intervention, like that of a musician

Scope and limits of aesthetic originality of Byzantine artists

performing a work by Mozart, never went beyond certain limits; to have transgressed them would have been disloyal to the Byzantine aesthetic canon. This is exactly what did happen, for example, in the works of Greek artists who, well after the fall of Byzantium, were influenced by Italian art.

We feel certain that the Byzantines of the Middle Ages owe the style of their works to religious ideas. It is above all in painting, which throughout the Middle Ages was the favourite medium of Byzantine artists, that one best realizes this, due to the great number of examples which have been preserved, and also because it was here more than in the other arts that one observes that major tendency of the Byzantines: to interpret the antique models handed down to them (cf. p. 121). One does indeed see them in perfect accord with Christian spirituality, attacking on the one hand everything which shows up to best advantage the substance, volume, weight, tactile values — and in a more general way the space, broken and un-broken, in which substance unfolds. Byzantine aesthetics also tend to reject the accidental, to ignore the instantaneous in order to maintain only the typical and the durable. In order to appreciate these values, enhanced through the eyes of faith because they draw nearer to the unalterability of things divine — this art made use of frank rhythm with a regular cadence, a purified line, restful sym-metries, a stability which cancels out contradictory movements. The eye is made to distinguish between these grave and harmonious images and the everyday material world, and to recognize in them the divine.

RELIGION AND PAINTING

To the extent that the aesthetics of a building can be compared with those of a painting or a bas-relief, we can allow ourselves to recognize parallel trends: a limpid composition, harmonious and restful balance, an overall symmetry and the absence of all tension, of all apparent effort. All this is unlike medieval Western architecture.

SPIRITUAL BASIS OF ARCHITECTURE

This form of aesthetics seems to us to rest on a religious basis, art reflecting the idea of divine perfection and of a vision of the irrational world into which the believer is transported by his faith. We know that the Byzantine religious edifice — the church in the shape of a cube surmounted by a hemispherical dome — has from the sixth century been compared to a microcosm (in a Syriac description of

'Microcosm' churches

the cathedral of St. Sophia in Edessa, which had this shape). Nothing better than this symbolic image can explain the tenacity with which the Byzantines held to this type of religious construction up to the end of the empire and even beyond.

Religious ideas and style of Byzantine images

On the other hand it may be suspected that Byzantine artists tended to express religious ideas through the aesthetic values of which we have just described certain principles. We have come to this conclusion by experiencing the effect these works have on us and also by observing the rigid system whereby, when it is a question of mosaics or frescoes, these pictures are placed close together, the order in which they follow one another and the way in which they are related to the architecture of the church microcosm. These paintings express the same idea in their own way, the microcosm being represented here both by the structure of the building with its domes and by a certain succession of images representing God and his faithful subjects in the cosmos, as well as the events of the Incarnation which made human beings citizens of the city of God.

The most perfect expression of these harmonious ensembles, both in architecture and in painting, date from the tenth and the eleventh centuries. They remained very fine in the twelfth century, although sometimes during the Comnenian period one feels that there were tendencies which might finally shatter the perfect balance attained in the works produced immediately before them. These trends were accentuated during the final Byzantine period, less in architecture than in the figurative arts, and even more particularly in painting. It would be far too easy to attribute them to external events, the most important fact in this connection being the arrival of Westerners in Byzantine territory and the frequent contacts of the Greeks with the Latins — with their form of worship, and also with their art, which had flourished since the twelfth century. But if this contact, which was maintained after the recapture of Constantinople by the Greeks in 1261, can explain many changes in the Byzantine works of this late period, the relationship cannot be established with certainty.

It was probably due to a far more complex process: the art of the Palaeologian period reflects in its way the Byzantine reaction to the events that occurred and the ideas that circulated at the end of the Middle Ages. What may in particular have been indirectly reflected in the religious art of the Byzantines of that period was increased national feeling due to contacts with Latins, Slavs and Turks, and on the religious plane with Roman Catholics and Muslims — the Greeks and the Orthodox in general being on the defensive and in a state of inferiority. It was within this framework that two tendencies appeared within Byzantine society, which were interpreted as opposed to one another. First of all there was a movement which idealized the national past and tried to revive its glories. This tendency was very marked under the Palaeologi and appeared in art in the form of more and more frequent imitations of ancient Greek models. We will return to this point a little later when dealing with all the 'renaissances' of this type which took place in Byzantine history.

Trend towards antiquity under Palaeologi

This movement towards a Greek revival seems to have been important at the beginning of the Palaeologian period. As in the case of all contemporary and similar movements in Italy and in France this movement towards ancient Greece was accompanied by an increased observation of reality. In the thirteenth and early fourteenth centuries the Byzantines attempted a movement in the same direction. But towards the middle of the fourteenth century there was a reaction, led by the Byzantine clergy and particularly by the monks, who being numerous and powerful exercised great influence in all strata of Byzantine society and could thus put a stop to this attempt at a more realistic form of art. No quest was undertaken in the opposite direction in order to express directly the ideas of this conservative movement, which might for example have meant a return to the grand style of the eleventh century. This movement, with its indifference to art, merely put a brake on all aesthetic research, whatever its object. At this point art remained static, rather like a language which has stopped developing at a moment when it was at its highest point, and was not without its contradictions. As always occurs in such cases, a sort of aesthetic compromise was reached which, more or less 'canonized', was used for several centuries in all sacred art of Greek and Slavonic Orthodox believers. We are of course dealing here with religious art, which undoubtedly played the main part in Byzantine art under the Palaeologi and of which we have more knowledge than of secular art. Here we must remind

Clerical reaction in XIVth century

ourselves that at that period the fate of the Byzantine state, which was definitely in decline from the beginning of the thirteenth century onwards, was very different from that of the Byzantine Church, which kept its prestige intact in the eyes of all the Orthodox peoples. During this period, and even after the fall of the empire of Constantinople, the Byzantine Church was responsible for a certain Byzantine universality. Thus the fate of Byzantine art followed that of the Church, not that of the state. This was of course due to the close bonds which linked art with worship; moreover, since art ignores linguistic barriers, it spread further and had a more immediate impact than any literary work whatever could have had. It was largely because art was in the service of the Church of Constantinople, which during that period entirely dominated all Byzantine monasteries, including Mount Athos, that we find in it practically no reflection of Latin aesthetics or iconography. This may seem surprising when we remember the many attempts made to obtain unity with the Roman Church, which resulted in agreements such as those reached at the Council of Lyons in 1274 or that of Florence in 1439. But on the Greek side these acts were the work of the emperors of Constantinople, who were followed by only a minute segment of the higher clergy, and that is why they had no effect. The ecclesiastical and political penetration of the Latins into Byzantine territory from the early thirteenth century onwards was largely responsible for this hostility. The conservatism of Byzantine art, which became systematic after the middle of the fourteenth century, was the price which it paid for its 'universality' and the longevity which it acquired from its close alliance with the Church. We shall see that the tiny portion of this art which tried to keep outside the mainstream of development soon came to reflect the various and contradictory influences which were met with at that period on the soil of the great empire of the past.

Universality of art allied to the Church

PLATE P. 21

INFLUENCE OF LITURGY ON ART

Amongst the religious factors which fashioned Byzantine art one was essential: liturgy. All monumental Christian art in Byzantium bears traces of the services celebrated in church, and this also applies to the essential parts of illustrated books and industrial luxury arts. But these links with church services could take various forms. In certain cases, as in the manuscripts of the Gospels known as liturgical

PLATE 13 – St. Gregory the Thaumaturge. Mosaic at Hosios Lucas in Phocis, *ca.* 1000. *Cf. p. 34*

PLATE 15 – The Prophet Jeremiah facing Christ. Miniature, *ca.* 1100. *Laurentian Library, Florence* (*P. 5.9.128*). *Cf. p. 173*

◀ PLATE 14 – The Archangel Michael. Roll of Joshua (detail), xth-century miniature. *Vatican Library* (*MS. Pal. Gr. 431*). *Cf. p. 168*

PLATE 16 – Two saints. Mosaic in the convent of Nea Moni on Chios, middle of xith century.
Cf. p. 34

66

PLATE 17 – Binding in silver gilt with raised relief work, xivth century. *Marcian Library, Venice. Cf. pp. 34, 50, 189*

PLATE 18 – St. Peter. Enamel on a chalice offered by the Emperor Romanus II (?), *ca.* 950. *Treasury of St. Mark's, Venice. Cf. pp. 33, 189*

PLATE 19 – The Archangel Gabriel. Detail of a miniature with portrait of the Emperor Nicephorus Botaniates, middle of xith century. *Bibliothèque Nationale, Paris (MS. Coislin 79). Cf. pp. 173, 175*

PLATE 20 – The Mother of God, Pentecost: mosaics in the apse and the dome which precedes it at
Hosios Lucas in Phocis, *ca.* 1000. *Cf. p. 34*

ones, the links are evident in the choice and order of the pictures, which represent the events commemorated by the feasts of the liturgical year and the order in which they are celebrated. Liturgical vases have a shape adapted to their use, and at times the iconographic images which decorate them are chosen so as to commemorate the founding of the sacrament of communion, or simply its founder, Jesus Christ. At other times the influence of ecclesiastical services is less direct, but no less present, as for example in the cycle of embroidered pictures on the sacred vestments of a Byzantine bishop or priest.

But this liturgical influence is of primary importance in all monumental art. Though less marked than in early Christian art, this influence is strong, but of varying intensity and scope.

Liturgy and monumental art

In Byzantine architecture, to which we shall return later, each building intended for worship was conveniently arranged for this purpose. Byzantine churches were turned to the East (with the usual variations we find in medieval art); the altar was placed in the middle of the choir towards the east, and was marked externally by a semi-circular or ribbed apse; the altar-table was fixed into the flagging and a passage was kept open between the altar and the rear wall of the apse. In episcopal churches we also find a synthronus — i.e., a bench which rests against the wall of the apse, where the clergy sat at certain times during the service, presided over by the bishop. More often, two smaller apses flank the main one — forming the east wall of the premises. These were used as follows: the one on the north for the preparation of the bread and wine, during the part of the mass called *proskomidi* — it is known as the *prothesis* (proposition), inspired by the proposition table of the biblical Temple — and the other, on the south side, is known as *diakonikon*, and was essentially used as a vestry and sacristy.

On the other hand, the Byzantine architects of the Middle Ages did not discover a way of completely separating those who officiated from those who worshipped. The partition of the iconostasis, called *templon* by the Greeks, was thin and for a long time rather low, being a piece of liturgical furniture rather than an element of architecture. The interior arrangements of a medieval church remained the same as during the paleo-Christian period; whereas the basilical form of the place of worship gave place to a building with a central plan dominated by a dome in the centre. Whatever explanation we may give of this (see below), this partial discord undoubtedly proves a certain conservatism on the part of the Byzantine architects of the Middle Ages, but does not compromise the principle that the liturgy always maintained an influence upon church architecture. Certainly the iconostasis was not well adapted to the general usefulness of a building with a central plan and a dome, but this merely emphasized the necessities of worship, which architects satisfied as best they could.

It is creations of the same origin which we are dealing with in the more important of the monastic churches, where apses were built into the two lateral walls — meant for two groups of cantors, and where the vestibules of the church were transformed into spacious chambers — because it was there that the monks celebrated a certain number of their secondary services.

Modest proportions of medieval Byzantine religious buildings This is perhaps the right place to mention a peculiarity of Byzantine religious architecture in the Middle Ages which distinguishes it both from the ecclesiastical architecture of antiquity in Byzantium and elsewhere as well as from the medieval churches of the West. In Byzantium medieval churches were never as large as the Christian basilicas built from the fourth to the sixth century or the churches of all the Latin countries from the Carolingian period onwards. It was not the requirements of the liturgical services which made the Byzantines keep to these modest proportions; instead they must have evolved progressively under the combined influence of the services and the technique of vaulted construction.

Even during antiquity, when basilicas were roofed with wood, the Byzantines constructed vaulted buildings with domes and put up baptisteries, mausoleums or *martyria*, which were derived from mausoleums and were used for the worship of relics. From the sixth century onwards the plans — square and rectangle, circle and polygon, cross — and the complete vaulting with a dome, which were the characteristics of mausoleums, *martyria* and baptisteries, were transferred to normal churches. In Byzantium and the surrounding area, which during the Middle Ages was to be the domain of Byzantine art proper, it was this type of small building, defined by a square plan, or one very close to it, with vaulting and a central dome, which was the one most often chosen of the various models. The conditions under which this transfer took place have not yet been cleared up. This is not so surprising when one bears in mind the lack of monuments and texts which survive from the period when this process took place. The hypothesis which seems the most plausible to us rests on the assumption that the commemorative sanctuaries, which during antiquity were *extra muros*, were subsequently transferred into the cities. This movement was a general one, which can be seen in Byzantium, Rome and elsewhere. But depending on the city and the district, church architecture was modified according to the ecclesiastical architecture of the country, the choice as always being conditioned by more than one factor.

Some of these factors are common to all countries. Thus the relative shortage of space in the cities may have contributed towards the disappearance of special buildings reserved for baptisms and the worship of relics, and to the moving of these services to the church itself. But in the West the suppression of autonomous baptisteries and *martyria* did not lead to the abandonment of the basilical shape of churches which catered to these special forms of worship. In Byzantium and Transcaucasia ecclesiastical buildings took on the shape of the *martyrium*, having adopted its liturgical functions, adding them to its own and those of the baptisteries. In the West, on the other hand, the same tendency, if it did not lead to the abandonment of the basilical type of church, endowed it with new elements designed to house relics and the commemorative services which were celebrated around them: crypts and chapels around the choir. As to what succeeded paleo-Christian baptisteries, neither in Byzantium nor in the West were they housed in any special place. It would appear that the custom of baptizing infants did away with the necessity for a special place where baptismal services could be held, since baptism no longer was a rarely celebrated ceremony attended by many people, but only by the young neophyte's family. This explains why it was the worship of relics rather than the baptismal rite which imposed its imprint on Christian architecture, though in a different way in the West than in Byzantium, in the period when antique religious edifices were being transformed into medieval churches.

However, in the case of Byzantium — which is alone of interest to us here — an ideological factor may have influenced the success of the cubic building with a dome, inspired by the architecture of the *martyria*. From the sixth century onwards this type of building was compared to a microcosm, its structure recalling that of the universe, as conceived by the cosmographers of the period. Once launched, this symbol was maintained, and during the Middle Ages the liturgists and the painters who decorated Byzantine churches continued to consider this type of building as a microcosm or an image of the Christian universe.

Symbolism of the microcosm

Certain historians of architecture, particularly those who lived at the beginning of this century, ignored the real and ideal functions of these religious buildings and, concentrating merely on their structure, saw in the Byzantine church of the Middle Ages a derivative of the sixth-century domed basilicas. There are very few buildings of this type (Philippi in Macedonia, Church B; Pirdop, in Bulgaria; St. Eirene in Constantinople), and they afford in our opinion very instructive evidence on the architecture of that fairly prolonged period (sixth–seventh centuries). It was difficult to reconcile the basilica which was being given up with the vaulting with a dome that was coming to be preferred for the roofing of ecclesiastical buildings. The fact is unwittingly confirmed by the hybrid buildings which we have just mentioned, the so-called domed basilicas. It would be better to regard these buildings, not as a particular type of church building, but as instructive evidence of the process which from the sixth century onwards gave Byzantine churches the appearance they were to have during the Middle Ages, and which borrowed its essential characteristics from the *martyrium* of late antiquity. In Transcaucasia ecclesiastical architecture went through similar stages, but with regional characteristics which were related not only to the various stages in the formation of medieval architecture, but also the shapes of the *martyria* which were known in this region.

General use of this type of building, with its system of vaulting topped by a central dome, meant not only that the builders had to have great knowledge of their craft, but also that religious buildings had to remain on a fairly small scale. To build any sort of a dome with surrounding vaults to support it, required certain technical knowledge — and the need for this was enormously increased in relation to the scale of the building. A craftsman might succeed in building a dome with a diameter of three or four metres, but could not possibly put up a larger one, nor establish the number or the size of the supports needed for this. The fact that technical difficulties increased in a geometrical ratio with the size of the building is a major reason why the Byzantine churches of the Middle Ages were generally small in size. The diminutive proportions always strike the Western observer, who should, however, remember that the generally large scale of Western churches was often an exaggeration in the opposite direction.

This tendency towards the 'colossal' came about during and after the Carolingian period, with the desire to imitate the vast Roman monuments — including the basilicas erected by Constantine and his immediate successors in Rome, Trier, Milan and elsewhere. The sight of these ruins of colossal buildings had a great effect in the West and as a result medieval architects sought to imitate them. If during the same period the Byzantines were disinclined to take this direction, this was probably due in part to the technical difficulties we have just mentioned. The case of Byzantium is all the more instructive in this respect, in that during the first flowering of Christian architecture under Justinian an attempt was made to apply the colossal Roman scale to churches. But precisely this experience brought out the difficulties of adhering to a vast scale when it was desired to put up entirely vaulted buildings. One has only to remember a few of the mishaps of the sixth-century Byzantine builders who applied this type of vaulting, including the large brick dome. The original dome and part of the vaulting of St. Sophia collapsed after a few years. It is rightly suspected that a similar collapse took place after the building of Church B at Philippi. For my part I am convinced that the dome of Pirdop did not stand up for very long either. Finally, in the case of St. Eirene, built a little later, we find ourselves in the presence of rather unfortunate vaulting which betrays the architects' groping efforts to attain solidity by multiplying the safeguards against collapse. All these precautionary measures closely linked to the technique of vaulting came into play when new churches were built in the ninth century under Theophilus and particularly the first Macedonians. These buildings were of far more modest proportions than those of the sixth century. The proportions established then remained standard up to the fall of Byzantium.

One might also ask whether economic factors were responsible for the small size of Byzantine churches. Did the shrunken empire possess the means to continue monumental art of gigantic proportions? But this argument is of no value. The Byzantine government of the Middle Ages and many private individuals possessed vast revenues, and we also know that they were able to spend enormous sums on rich decoration and furnishings for their churches — preferring to spend their money in this way rather than on large-scale constructions. Nor should we blame the absence of large buildings on the lack of qualified architects. It is of course true that no names of medieval Byzantine architects have come down to us, and another fact which may be disturbing was that at the beginning of the eleventh century it was an Armenian architect who was summoned to Constantinople to repair the dome of St. Sophia. Should we not deduce from this that in Constantinople under the last Macedonians there was a lack of sufficiently qualified technicians? While this point might possibly be conceded, we must be careful not to make out of this incident a generalized theory and to apply it to the entire medieval period. This is borne out particularly by one fact which proves that there existed Byzantine architects eminently qualified to put up large-scale buildings. We know that the Turkish invaders called upon Greek architects when, shortly after the conquest of Constantinople in 1453, they undertook the building of several monumental mosques. These buildings were on the scale of the largest vaulted churches of the sixth century, which proves that there were Greek architects capable of executing them, and also of reviving the colossal scale of St. Sophia or the Holy Apostles. We must also add that in the countries they converted — first Bulgaria and then Russia — the Byzantines in the tenth and eleventh centuries put up churches far larger than those they built in their own country — for example, the basilica of Pliska and St. Sophia in Kiev.

Once they got away from their attempts to imitate the colossal scale of the Romans, which Justinian had continued to do, they built churches on a scale commensurate with what circumstances required. Where we have texts to help us we can see that these churches were designed for communities of monks and nuns whose numbers were small and who had no need of large buildings. This also applied to Mount Athos, particularly before the fall of the Empire, despite the fame of the Holy Mountain. This example and those of other 'holy mountains' such as Mount Olympus in Bithynia, Mount Parnassus in Boeotia, on the island of Euboea, etc. can tell us much about the practice of Greek cenobism, which preferred numerous autonomous monastic installations, each possessing its own church, to the practice of having crowds of faithful gather around a single church within the conventual enclosure. On Mount Athos there are not one, but twenty important convents; and around several of them are other monastic establishments which topographically and architecturally, if not administratively, are independent, in that each possesses its own church.

This system favoured small-scale architecture, whereas the great monastic communities of the Latin world put up far larger churches, for reasons unconnected with the Roman tradition of the colossal. These proportions, as we know, increased even further when the nave of the church was divided into two separate parts, one for the monks and one for the laity.

This type of openly admitted separation never existed in the liturgical practices of the Byzantine Church, which in all matters laid down the law far less strictly than did the Latin Church. There is no evidence that at any period crowds of pilgrims were ever herded into a secondary part of an Athonite church. But in St. Sophia the faithful always remained in the side aisles, and other restrictions of the same sort may have existed elsewhere — particularly in monastic and urban churches, where we find large vestibules, which either precede or surround the three sides of the actual church. The development of these exterior areas should perhaps be related, at least in part, to the intention of reserving for the monks and other important persons the nave of the church, while keeping other people in the annexes.

There is a last category of important ideas which were firmly anchored in the Byzantine consciousness, stimulated their artistic activities and influenced a great many of their artistic works during the Middle Ages. I am thinking of humanism — that is to say an admiration for everything derived from classical Greece: language, literature, science and art. In the intellectual circles of Constantinople everything which came from the ancient Greeks was appreciated and imitated, and this 'archaeological' trend became even more widespread from the ninth century onwards, at a time when aesthetic preoccupations also became more involved with national passions. Finally it was in the glories of the past, as had often been the case, that the Greeks of the Palaeologian period looked for and found moral support. One must not imagine, of course, that this taste for ancient Greece allowed the Byzantines to bring their literature and their science to the level it had enjoyed in the past. But their efforts were praiseworthy, if only because they preserved from oblivion the heritage of the past and at the same time acknowledged a taste for beauty and certain fundamental rules of classical aesthetics. It must be said that here too there was a great deal of mere rhetoric, and the Church for its part laid down narrow limits to this outburst of Christian 'humanism'. Nevertheless, the fact remains that down the ages Byzantine artists were attracted to the works of art of their distant ancestors, and that in copying, imitating and gaining inspiration from these works they gave their own paintings and sculpture the imprint of the classical tradition. This was one of the invariable factors in medieval Byzantine art and a source of inspiration which the Greek artists of that period knew how to cultivate systematically and with greater understanding than their fellow artists of the West did at that time.

There were, however, periods more or less favourable to these adaptations of ancient art which did not manifest themselves in the same way in all fields of artistic activity. Thus the first important classical movement dates from the tenth century and continued on to the eleventh. It was a period when the court was very receptive to 'humanist' ideas, which were especially encouraged by the

Emperor Constantine VII Porphyrogenitus. Figurative arts and particularly manuscript paintings reflected this same taste. In them we can admire pictures which are perfect imitations of models of the fourth and fifth centuries. The ease with which the tenth-century Byzantine painters adapted themselves to a style created five centuries earlier is astonishing. One learns at the same time the approximate date of their models and one deduces that what these artists brought back to life was already a Christian antiquity. It was the period which for them represented the whole of the classical age. Natural as this may seem, that age being closer to them in time and in its ideas, one is pleased to learn this because at the same time one realizes far better what the work of this last Greek period was able to teach the Byzantine artists of the Middle Ages.

Christian antiquity as a model for artists

After this first movement, which had far less influence on mural paintings and mosaics than on miniatures and ivory sculptures, there may have been a lull. But the Greek offensive started up again during the Comnenian era in the twelfth century, and perhaps a little earlier. Amongst the accomplishments of the Comnenian period we no longer find copies of Greek works so accurate that they could sometimes deceive the expert, but rather a reappraisal of style. The human face, drapery and the composition as a whole reached a perfect balance which must have required long studies of proportion, of the rhythm of lines and volumes, of the power of expression of a silhouette against a plain background. This research was based on a careful study of classical models, particularly sculpture. It is in these compositions, as in certain carefully executed architectural works of that period, that one discovers a great many applications of the Golden Number, which proves that the artists enjoyed an advanced theoretical education. They also introduced into their works whole motifs lifted from the Greeks — naked bodies, standing or recumbent — as in the Crucifixion or the Descent into Limbo in the mosaics at Daphni.

Character of imitations from the antique during XIIth century

In many of the eleventh- and twelfth-century monuments we often notice attempts to reproduce one particular Greek motif, which after being touched up is then incorporated in a context of Christian imagery. But before the second half of the twelfth century we have only isolated motifs and elements, which decorated but did not emphasize the figuration. However, this did take place a little later, from the end of the twelfth century onwards and particularly during the reign of the Palaeologi, in the thirteenth and fourteenth centuries. The art produced then was more lively, more sensitive to emotion and drama; it was more conversational, whether its language was descriptive, lyrical or personal. In order to produce a better and more emotional description it went back for inspiration to nature and to the various earlier experiments of Greek art. From this the artists borrowed not only typical draped figures with their expressive and elegant gestures, but formulas of typical movements, backgrounds of landscapes with rocks and architectural elements which clear out a certain space around the figures in action. The Greek contribution extended to costumes, personifications and entire landscapes. The extent of these contributions was far greater than in the past, and seemed better assimilated. Instead of being superimposed on medieval elements, these Greek motifs permeate them.

The Greek contribution (XIIth–XIVth centuries)

Any Byzantine painting executed around 1300 gives proof of this, with its light and jagged architectural landscape, its vela suspended from imaginary temples and the frequent personifications, the animated and graceful scenes which were enacted there — all this reminds us at times of the orginal revival of what is called Pompeian painting. This is of course only a passing phase — because the art of the Palaeologi was far from being a simple return to the art of the first centuries, but the imprint of the Byzantine humanism of that period can really be felt.

It is not by chance that the most beautiful Byzantine monuments of the period — the church of Christ in Chora in Constantinople, with its mosaics and its frescoes — was initiated by Theodore Metochites, a great scholar of Greek science and literature. The two forms of Byzantine art visibly went together; and as far as the paintings in the church of Christ in Chora are concerned, the slightly precious side which astonishes us in an ecclesiastical work of art finds its counterpart in the humanist literature of the period. Just as the elegant martyrs are dressed as pages or ephebes on the mosaics of the church of Christ in Chora, so we find a literature that is a hothouse art. It contains no hint of the catastrophic position of Byzan-

Church of Christ in Chora (Kariye Camii) in Constantinople
PLATE P. 92

tium. One would expect to find religious art echoing a period of distress; instead we have pleasing pictures.

We ought to end this rapid survey of the ideas from which Byzantine art drew its inspiration by recalling a few secondary sources that should not be neglected. Their influence is seen in secular art. At the imperial court luxury trades were practised, such as the weaving of silk and gold threads, embroidery, precious metal-work of all kinds, and work on ivory — because these rare and precious objects pleased the princes and added to their prestige. This was the case in other medieval kingdoms as well, and the Byzantines wished to take the lead. However, this same political background also gave birth to certain cycles of images of the princely cycle, starting with portraits of rulers shown in a light dictated by doctrine. In this field, too, classical Greece had something to contribute to the Middle Ages, but it was the extreme end of antiquity, the Roman Empire after its conversion, which gave medieval Byzantium its formulas and symbols of power. They were enriched by new elements from the Oriental kingdoms, first Iranian, then Arab and Turkish. Had the Great Byzantine Palace been preserved, it would have revealed many treasures having as a background the political ideas of which these arts were the symbols.

As well as this the imperial palace and all the princely Byzantine courts of the Middle Ages maintained permanent contact with all the Western European courts. For a long time it was the latter who sought the favour of Byzantium. But from about the eleventh century onwards this was no longer necessarily so, and little by little, during the period of the Crusades and later, Byzantine society had to take into account the customs and arts which flourished in the castles and cities of the Latin world — first treating them as equals and eventually having to seek their favour. The secular art of the Western world penetrated fairly extensively into Byzantium. In this field it is perhaps difficult to speak of an ideology. But despite this, the influence of the customs and the arts of the Latin world testify, although not systematically, to the fact that elements of Latin civilization filtered into the secular world of Byzantium, particularly during the Palaeologian period.

When one is dealing with an art which flourished over several centuries, in a state so important as the Byzantine Empire, and over a territory which for a long time was immense (contrary to what is often claimed), it must be emphasized that Byzantine works of art were very varied.

One of the reasons for the richness of this repertory and its intentions stems from the variety of ideas which Byzantine work was called upon to represent. Some of these were definitely Byzantine, others were brought in from elsewhere or borrowed from an already distant past. These dissimilar ideas found expression in various distinctive forms which existed side by side within Byzantine works of art.

PART II

A HISTORICAL GLIMPSE
OF MEDIEVAL BYZANTINE ART

NOTE

There are several possible ways of presenting the most typical characteristics of the history of Byzantine art. We have chosen a simple and unoriginal plan, which, however, we will not stick to too rigidly, so that the works of art may speak for themselves and reduce to a minimum those deceptive barriers which stem from over-rigid classification. In most cases architecture, figurative and ornamental arts are best studied together. But in other cases monumental and other arts are different and one gains by treating them separately. This is what we shall do for the works of the Palaeologian period.

Guided by the monuments which remain and by the great events of history which exercised a definite influence on the arts, we shall in turn look at:

i.   art during the Iconoclast period; architecture, figurative and ornamental art;

ii. the upsurge of this art after the Iconoclast crisis and the important stages in its history up to the fall of Byzantium;

iii. architecture from the ninth to the fifteenth century;

iv. painting, sculpture and the ornamental arts from the end of Iconoclasm to the sack of Constantinople by the Crusaders in 1204;

v.   the figurative arts from the thirteenth to the fifteenth century.

I. ART DURING THE REIGN
OF THE ICONOCLASTS (726-843)

It was in 726 that Emperor Leo III, the Isaurian, published the first decree against icons, and had the picture of Christ which was over the door of the Imperial Palace destroyed. The deep causes of this official and open struggle by the government of the empire of Constantinople against images do not concern us here, nor do the external events of history. Nowadays some historians tend to minimize the importance of this 'quarrel over images', when set against the whole governmental policy of Leo III and his successors (who were also hostile to images). One would certainly be wrong to forget, in particular, the decisive efforts which they made to resist the onslaught of Islam, as well as the close relationship there was between the defence of the Byzantine state, whose very existence was at stake, and the Iconoclast policy of the emperors. This policy drew them closer to their subjects in Asia Minor, who were in the forefront of the battle and hostile to religious images. It also drew them closer to the Muslims and might have impaired the resistance of the Christians in Asia Minor to Muslim attacks. But while one may in general concede that the Iconoclasm of these emperors was not the main characteristic of their policy, in the field of art the rejection and prohibition of religious images was of supreme importance.

For the art historian the emperors who reigned in the eighth and the first half of the ninth century did nothing more important than to forbid religious images. Thus they well deserve the name which their Orthodox enemies gave them, all the more so because the liquidation of the movement, as well as the movement itself, had numerous important repercussions on the fate of medieval Byzantine religious art. It is above all of these consequences that we must speak here, leaving aside all that concerns the development of the crisis over images, from the events of 726 referred to above to the definite abandonment of official iconophobia by the emperors, which took place in the spring of 843 and was celebrated in Byzantium as the 'Triumph of the Orthodox'. Between these dates there was a period of calm which corresponds to the reigns of three Orthodox sovereigns (780–813). In 787 the Seventh Oecumenical Council decided upon a return to the use of holy images and authorized their veneration. But although the decisions of the Council remained valid within the Universal Church, they were rejected in 813 by Leo v, the Armenian, and by his two immediate successors, Michael ii and above all Theophilus. It was only after his death that his wife Theodora definitely restored the use and cult of icons.

THE
ICONOCLAST
BASILEIS

The Iconoclasts would have no place in the history of art if their activities in that field had been limited only to the destruction of images. But this was not so. Firstly their prohibition extended only to religious images, and not to all images. They were even accused of prolonging the use of imperial effigies, figures of themselves and

Numismatic
imperial effigies

members of their families. On their coins one can even observe a tendency to show side by side (on both faces of the coin) as many as three or four generations of the princes of their family, who reigned successively. It is obvious that on the political plane these sovereigns used such coins as propaganda for their dynasty. In this sense they went even further than their predecessors, and this clearly emphasizes the demarcation line between what the emperors thought it permissible to represent and what they did not. As we see, only Christian religious imagery was forbidden; and numismatics indirectly confirm this, as Iconoclast coins never show the effigy of Christ, as did those of Justinian ii (685–711), their immediate predecessor, but it reappears directly after the end of the Iconoclast crisis in 843 on the issues of the first Orthodox *basileus*, Michael iii.

One also learns, through the writings of the enemies of the Iconoclasts, that in the churches where sacred images were stamped out one could still find trees, plants of all kinds, vegetable gardens and even aviaries — that is to say, birds among plants. In one public

Decoration of secular
images in churches

building, the 'Milion', pictures of the Councils were replaced by those of a horse-race in the Hippodrome. All these subjects, some of which were aniconic, do not seem to have been invented by the Iconoclasts. It was rather a revival of decoration without figures, such as one could see before in the paleo-Christian churches (for example in Aquileia and Padua), and again with the Arabs (for example in Damascus, where the artists must have copied a Byzan-

PLATE 21 – Communion of the Apostles (detail). Mural painting in the rock-cut church of Karabas-Kilise, Cappadocia, 1060. *Cf. p. 34*

PLATE 22 – Hezekiah, king of Judah, on his sick-bed. Detail of miniature from a psalter, first half of xth century. *Bibliothèque Nationale, Paris (MS. Grec 139). Cf. p. 170*

88

PLATE 23 – The Virgin in Paradise. The convent of Bačkovo, in the south of Bulgaria. Mural painting, *ca.* 1100.

PLATE 24 – The Ascension (detail). Mosiac at St. Sophia, Salonika, end of ixth century. *Cf. pp. 122, 13.*

PLATE 25 – History of the Apostles Peter and Paul. Mosaic in the collaterals of the aisle of the Palatine Chapel in Palermo, *ca.* 1160. *Cf. p. 149*

PLATE 26 – Joseph reproaching Mary on seeing her with child. Mosaic at Kariye Camii, Istanbul, *ca.* 1320. *Cf. p. 80*

PLATE 27 – The Baptism. Mosaic at Hosios Lucas in Phocis, *ca.*1000. *Cf. p. 143*

PLATE 28 — St. Mark the Evangelist. Detail of a miniature from the Xth century. Biblioteca Medicea-Laurenziana, Florence.

tine model belonging to the same tradition). In the same way hunting and fishing scenes decorated churches of the fourth century, as we learn from a letter written by St. Nilus. Finally, pictures of the races in the Hippodrome had occurred since the Roman period, either on official monuments such as the diptychs of the Consuls, where New Year's Day races were shown, or in houses and objects belonging to private individuals. The latter pictures portray a well-known driver or a favourite horse, unless they were used as *apotropaia* as was often the case.

At any rate one learns that the hostility of the Iconoclasts extended only to religious images and except in this domain they allowed and even encouraged the representation of personages, those of the imperial period and those that had traditionally been treated in secular art from the end of antiquity up to the beginning of the Iconoclast period.

The last Iconoclast emperor, Theophilus, had a taste for luxury and buildings. He also had more opportunities to indulge this taste as a result of the first victories over the Arabs. We thus see him erecting buildings in his palace in Constantinople and reviving the former splendours of the symbolic court ceremonies, filling his palace with luxurious furniture, gold plate and a great variety of ceremonial dress, worn by his court officials. Witnesses have stated that Theophilus was dazzled by the splendour of the houses of the Abassid caliphs in Baghdad and probably intended to outdo them for reasons of political prestige. Little or nothing is known of what all these works created upon the initiative of Theophilus were like, but there are indications which lead us to suspect the influence of Arab princes on the art of the court. Thus in the palace he built, not a large single construction, as had been done in earlier palaces, but separate independent pavilions, which were given names, such as 'Pearl', that make one think of the kiosks in the gardens of Muslim rulers.

Art under the last Iconoclast emperor Theophilus

If, as local tradition has it, the fragment of silk decorated with pictures of unknown Byzantine emperors hunting a lion, today in the Silk Museum in Lyons, was truly a gift of the Iconoclast emperor Constantine V (741–775) to the abbey of Mozac in Auvergne, we are in possession here of an authentic work from the imperial work-

A textile of the Iconoclast period

shops during the Iconoclast period. The picture of the mounted emperor spearing the lion appears very Persian; it is merely an adaptation to the person of the Byzantine emperor of figures which were common in Sassanid Persia, and which were repeated again in Iran and the adjoining area under the first Muslim dynasties — and in fact were contemporary with the Byzantine textile at Mozac. We also have a text written by Patriarch Nicephorus at the beginning of the ninth century in which it is said that pictures of animals and perhaps monsters decorated iconostases in the churches of his time. According both to Patriarch Nicephorus' text and to the ornamentation and style of the human and animal figures which we admire on these textiles of the Iconoclast period, the works created at that time show Oriental, Persian and Arab influences. Besides we know that the caliphs of the seventh and eighth centuries, contemporaries of the Iconoclast emperors, for their part encouraged a court art in which Syro-Hellenic, Roman and Iranian-Sassanid elements were closely knit together to produce decoration of sur-

Monumental decoration on carpets in relief

prising richness. The monumental decorations of carpets with relief, delicately traced, developed boldly the efforts previously made by the Sassanids and probably under their influence by the Byzantines, in the century of Justinian. One finds similar ornamental carpets in Byzantium at the end of the Iconoclast crisis, but incorporated into the decoration of manuscripts and architectural pottery. It is probable that these are continuations of what had been produced there even at the time of the quarrel over images. But it would be going too far to attribute to the Iconoclasts the introduction to Byzantium of increased Iranian influence. It is far more consistent with what we know about them to imagine them — like the caliphs, their contemporaries — prolonging in the realm of art what was already there, apart from figurative religious images. Except for the problem of icons, which they rejected, they do not seem to have been very preoccupied with art. It could also be that the Oriental elements, so numerous in the sculptured and painted ornaments of the first decades after the Triumph of the Orthodox in 843, were not introduced by the Iconoclasts, but were a prolongation of the great Byzantine tradition of the sixth century which included ornamental carpets and Iranian motifs.

We do not have to occupy ourselves here with the theological basis of the dispute which in the eighth and ninth centuries raged in Byzantium — the quarrel between the defenders and adversaries of icons, that is to say, representations of Christ and the saints or scenes in which divine personages or saints appear. What counted in the practice of the arts was not the learned doctrines of the two groups, but violent opinions capable of upsetting the conscience of each individual, and official legislation accompanied by violence. Some ended up by leaning towards the Iconophobes, as they had a horror of idolatry; others held on to holy images, as these put into a concrete form the divine and the saintly which held such a great place in their lives, and they did not know how wholly to separate the representation from the subject represented. These difficulties had always existed, but they did not make themselves felt strongly until the imperial decrees forced everyone either to take up a position for or against the empire, or quietly to follow the legislators. There were convinced believers and opportunists, as well as martyrs on each side. The situation was made even more confused by the fact that the Orthodox Church only announced its decision half a century after the beginning of the crisis (at the Council of 787, confirmed in 842), whereas within the empire the decisions of the councils of the heretic church were reckoned to be the views of orthodoxy.

II. THE UPSURGE AFTER THE ICONOCLAST CRISIS AND THE MAIN STAGES IN ART HISTORY TO THE FALL OF BYZANTIUM

In 843 the crisis was ended, as it had started, by the decision of a sovereign. But a period of adjustment of about a quarter of a century was necessary before there could be a return to the use and veneration of images. The long period of Iconoclast 'orthodoxy' had had its effect upon the hearts and minds of the people. It also appears that there was a lack of technicians, or at any rate of artisans, for the more difficult work such as figurative mosaics applied to the vaults of churches.

The 'Macedonian renaissance' In actual fact the great period of Byzantine art only began with the advent of the first emperor of the so-called Macedonian dynasty, Basil I (867–886); this was the period which saw the growth of all types and techniques of figurative painting and certain aspects of sculpture, as well as of architecture and the decorative arts. Thus it is right to call this art which grew up after the definite condemnation of Iconoclasm 'the Macedonian renaissance'. Later on we shall see that the term 'renaissance' may be applied to this art only in some of its branches, specifically in the sense of a revival of Greek art. But for the moment it is a question of the general upsurge of artistic activity under the first emperors of the Macedonian dynasty. This movement was related to other developments in the fields of Byzan-

From the height of the Xth century to the sack of Constantinople by the Crusaders tine literature, science and technology. The tenth century was the climax of Byzantine civilization, and this great period continues into the second half of the eleventh century. Political, economic, religious, military and social life then went through a difficult period and important changes of all kinds took place: in 1054 there was a definite breach between the Church of Constantinople and that of Rome, which had the whole of Western Christendom behind her; in 1071 occurred the disastrous defeat of the Byzantines at Mantzikert in Armenia by the Seljuk Turks and the loss of the greater part of Asia Minor, which was never wholly reconquered; there was an increasing enslavement of the peasant masses and the rise of great aristocratic families, who were powerful landowners; and finally

98

the advent of the Comnenian dynasty (Alexius I, 1081–1118), the rule of which lasted almost throughout the twelfth century up to the sack of Constantinople by the Crusaders in 1204.

All these events and changes in the political and social structure of the empire were part of its history. But so far as one can see they had no important repercussions on the arts, and thus we cannot consider the works of the Macedonian and Comnenian periods in two separate chapters.

Certainly there were some notable developments and changes, more or less marked in one or another branch of art, within the long period which extends from about 865 to 1204 and includes the successive reigns of the Macedonians, their immediate successors and the Comneni, followed by several Angeli. It is enough to remember that the twelfth century was the age when Byzantine art spread beyond the frontiers of the empire, to an extent never surpassed before or after. It was then that Byzantine objects were to be found all over Western Europe as well as in all the countries of Eastern Europe. But it was also the first period of frequent and important penetration by Westerners into traditionally Byzantine countries, a movement which began with the Crusades. Most of the Holy Land was at that time in the hands of Latin Christians.

The twelfth century is traditionally categorized by reference to events from religious, military and social history which are hardly, if at all, reflected in an analysis of Byzantine works of art of this period. Architecture, the techniques of painting, sculpture limited to relief, and various kinds of luxury arts continued in the twelfth century, without undergoing any radical changes compared with the work done in the eleventh century. It would of course be inexact to say that there were only differences and variations, the basis remaining everywhere identical. A sort of cursive script was evolved in the twelfth century for use in mural paintings and even in miniatures. The object of this was to be able to work faster and produce more for sale. This had a reaction upon style, and not only in the negative sense — for in these works, which had to be executed rapidly, there was a true elegance. But in the middle of the twelfth century another tendency appeared which forecast the original work of the Palaeologian period with its new approach in the field of painting and sculpture; this consisted of a third dimension, an intensity of expression, a sense of the dramatic and the emotional, and an increase of realistic detail in order to produce an impression of truth. All this, of course, with the implicit intention of injecting concrete life into symbols.

From 1204 to the return of the Byzantines (1261)

This was the stage which had been reached when in 1204, after the celebrated sack of Constantinople, the Crusaders made it for more than half a century the capital of a Latin Empire. Apart from a few miniatures we have no idea of the art which was practised in Constantinople between 1204 and 1261, the date of the return of the Byzantines, who from then on were governed by emperors of the Palaeologian dynasty. But works of art created by Byzantine artists and their local followers in the thirteenth century in the small autonomous Greek states (Epirus, Macedonia) as well as in Serbia and Bulgaria give us an idea of the state of Byzantine art at the time of the Latin Empire, but perhaps only of that done outside the Latin state itself.

Art of the Palaeologi

Then with the Palaeologi in Constantinople and shortly afterwards in Mistra, the capital of a Byzantine province south of the Peloponnese, but also in other parts of the Balkan peninsula which were either Byzantine or were governed by Serbian or Bulgarian princes, a similar form of art became established; it is this art which we call the art of the Palaeologi. As many works have been preserved, we are in a position to study its evolution and particularities, which are the mark of the various workshops and the individual artists concerned. Alongside the religious branch, the main one, there also existed a secular one, which to begin with was more original, but around 1350 became conservative and remained so up to the end of the Byzantine period proper, which we, in accordance with the general view, date from the fall of the empire of Constantinople and the capture of the capital by the Osmanli Turks in 1453.

A detailed history of Byzantine art from its upsurge in the second half of the ninth century to the end of the empire in 1453 could either be divided into many distinct chapters or treated as a whole. As our text is brief we shall adopt the following method: we will present all architectural monuments in one single chapter. The stability of monumental art between the ninth and fifteenth centuries allows us to do so — and in this way it will be easier to appreciate the absence of an evolution through successive stages, which is one of the characteristics of Byzantine architecture. It is a question here only of religious architecture, as civil and military architecture have so far not been studied seriously.

Due to the volume of surviving works, their variety and the numerous changes, we have been forced to present figurative art — painting and sculpture — and decorative art in several chapters.

III. ARCHITECTURE FROM
THE NINTH TO THE FIFTEENTH CENTURY

GENERAL   In Byzantine countries, as everywhere around the Mediterranean, the great majority of remaining medieval buildings are works of religious architecture. It is churches and mosques that chiefly represent for us the architecture of the Middle Ages. The main reason for this is that secular buildings were treated with less regard and were more readily destroyed than religious ones. But it is also true that everywhere medieval society reserved to religion a preponderant part in the artistic activities it encouraged.

Byzantium followed this general rule, although the monarchs of Roman and Greek tradition attached particular importance to all that concerned the imperial palace, including its architecture. But little or nothing remains to us of the imperial palaces of Constantinople, and this gap — greater in Byzantium than elsewhere — is a considerable handicap to all who study Byzantine art. In the Middle Ages particularly the main buildings which comprised the Great Palace of the Emperor, of which we possess written descriptions, must have been closely related to religious buildings: their plans, their arches, their polychrome decorations of marble and mosaic lead us to picture rooms that were like the churches of the same period. This secular architecture of the monarchs surely has its counterpart in Byzantine religious architecture, as was the case in the West, where religious and secular architecture frequently made use of the same plans, and the same methods of building and roofing. But in both instances secular and religious architecture each display different characteristics.

BYZANTINE   What are the most striking features of Byzantine buildings?
CHURCHES   Byzantine churches are built of brick and rough or cut stone. In the Middle Ages the medium or small bond was definitely used more often than the large bond. Generally speaking, the choice between brick and stone as the principal material varies according to the district concerned: in Constantinople, Thessalonica, Macedonia and Asia Minor it was brick that dominated, whereas stone predominated

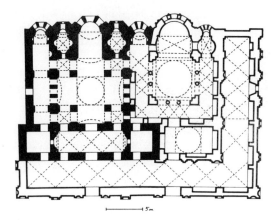

in most areas of continental Greece, including Athens and Mistra. But it is better to note that the simultaneous use of brick and stone was particularly favoured by Byzantine builders, the proportion of one to the other varying endlessly. Even where brick predominated, as in Constantinople, the foundations and framework of openings might be of cut stone; conversely, in buildings mainly of stone the arches and vaults, and sometimes the horizontal clampings which ran across the walls, were of brick.

Simultaneous use of brick and stone

This use of two different materials is easily explained: reasons of economy dictated use of the rough-cut stone to be found here and there. Elsewhere brick predominated, especially in urban areas. Wherever possible, enough bricks were procured to build the arches and vaults and to make straight walls more solid by the use of brick clampings.

The alternation of red brick and stone of more or less light colour also produced a decorative effect on church exteriors. Byzantine architects realized this and from the eleventh century to the end of the empire often made use of this method to obtain the maximum effect. It may be seen above all in the Palaeologian period, when the play of alternating colours on facades with ornamental motifs was enhanced by the use of bricks: cornices, tympani, cylindrical walls and apses often had this decoration in brick sunk into the mortar.

In the Palaeologian period glazed green or brown tiles (rows of little discs and rosettes sunk into the mortar) were also used to decorate façades.

As has been said in the introduction, the vast majority of medieval Byzantine churches were fairly small buildings. The reduced size certainly made building easier, as it did the vaulting which was usually used in churches. But certain skilful methods of building were applied to domes and vaults in all churches, including the most modest chapels. All these vaults, as well as groined arches and barrel vaults, were built 'without soffits' — that is to say, without the use of a provisional wooden framework to hold together the bricks (or stones) of an arch or vault during construction until the moment the mortar set. This skilled technique, like all the techniques and other practices used by Byzantine architects of the Middle Ages, had been handed down to them by their predecessors. In its essential characteristics their art was a continuation of that which flowered in Byzantium from as early as the fifth and sixth centuries. Thus one can see that two general types of plan and elevation

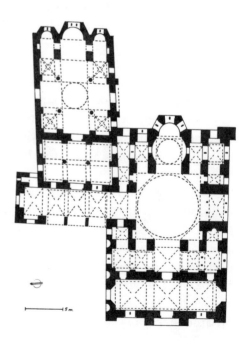

2 – Hosios Lucas in Phocis

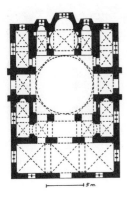

appear in medieval Byzantine churches. In fact we find the basilica roofed in wood and vaulted and the cubic building entirely vaulted and crowned by a central dome. It is true that from the numerical point of view the two types differ: there are very few medieval Byzantine basilicas, and those that we have are in a way really survivals from an earlier period. The vast majority are cubes surmounted by a dome: this was the favourite and most usual type for medieval Byzantine places of worship. For this reason a few words on basilicas will suffice. In the ninth as in the tenth century, that is to *Basilicas* say at the time of the 'renaissance' which followed Iconoclasm, the basilica form was still in use, probably in the same way as the various archaisms that one sees in the painted manuscripts of that time. In particular in the Byzantine provinces and in the neighbouring countries which imitated Byzantium, churches copying paleo-Christian basilicas with wooden roofs were built or re-built. Here are some examples: the cathedrals of Serres, Trikkala and Mesem- APPX. PL. I, 2 bria, the monastic church of St. Nicon at Sparta (foundations only), Pliska (foundations) and the island of St. Achilles on the lake of Prespa (the last two were founded by the Bulgar kings). So it occurs that in more than one Byzantine town of the Middle Ages the oldest church was a basilica, whereas the others were smaller, of cubic shape with a dome. Arta in Epirus, Kastoria in western Macedonia and Mesembria on the Black Sea are intermediate examples be-tween both types: they are later and smaller medieval vaulted basilicas. They are like truly medieval copies of the Byzantine

4 – Kapnikarea, Athens

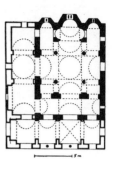

basilica; their reduced size and their vaulting link them with the other ecclesiastical buildings of the Middle Ages.

Buildings with central dome All other Byzantine sanctuaries fall into the great category of buildings with a central dome, which may be subdivided into several groups according to the following characteristics: domes with pendentives or on squinches, or a central dome flanked by four others, barrel vaults and groined arches around domes; the presence or absence of a bay sandwiched in between the apses and the square chamber surmounted by the dome; the presence or absence of vestibules and lateral galleries. We need not describe each of these APPX. PL. 3,12 particular types of Byzantine church, especially as it was not a question of fixed rules, but of varying interpretations of each of the essential characteristics of these churches. In practice each building presented a distinct combination of these characteristics and it would not be erroneous to classify them into definite categories.

However, Gabriel Millet is probably right to consider the presence of a supplementary bay in front of the apses and the frequent resort to groined arches to cover the compartments of the squinches around the dome, as trade-marks of the builders of Constantinople and their disciples. He also recognizes as originating in Constantinople works which, when viewed from the outside, show a clarity of design — jutting-out cornices, pilasters and blind arches — which allow one to recognize the interior construction of the building. But these observations, though useful, are only suggestive. There is nothing absolute about them and proof of this is that those who

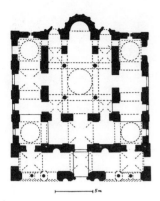

disagree are not necessarily wrong. In fact there are to be found in the same place and the same period churches with none of the characteristics of the Constantinople style, set among buildings of that type (cf. church of the Transfiguration in Athens, of St. John the Theologian at Mesembria, etc.). Built of quarry-stone, with façades which indicate poorly the interior layout of the building, deprived of all articulated plastic decor, these churches none the less belong to the Constantinople school. So one must not try to discover a style opposed to the latter, nor to define it as 'Oriental', a term that could be stretched to mean 'born and practised in the provinces east of Constantinople' (especially as we do not have any surviving buildings of this type). Nor is the style an aesthetic category separate from that of Constantinople which might reflect Hellenic taste, the classical tradition being characterized by a freedom of method and balance between the construction and the exterior appearance (see above). Interesting as speculations of this type might be, they could depend only in small part on the study of monuments, and here we do not wish to go beyond what we can actually see.

Thus if one is going to adhere to this wise principle one should not classify medieval Byzantine churches into two opposed groups. These two supposed groups are merely theoretical; reality is far more complex. So it is better to consider the monuments one after the other, or in small groups comprising those that are alike or closely related. Study of this kind brings out better the individual character

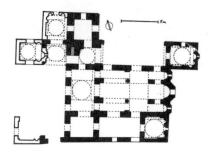

of each building. In addition to looking at works which still exist and continue to influence us as works of art, it will be sufficient to make a few remarks about the most usual features of this architecture in general. To those mentioned above we must add a final one that is of interest as it betrays a voluntary step forward and thus shows deliberate intent.

Byzantine churches, cubes with domes, have a number of clear variations inside: a dome with pendentives and four supports, a dome on squinches and eight supports, the presence or absence of galleries, a variety of secondary vaults and the height at which they are started. Certain of these methods, like the two types of dome, represent different traditions, and each comes from a different example (for instance the dome with squinches on eight supports must come from octagonal rooms contained in a cubic building). A medieval church at Peristera near Thessalonica preserves inside all the essential characteristics of a polygonal rotunda. However — and this is the constant mark of Greek ecclesiastical buildings of the Middle Ages, whatever their interior construction — they always present the external aspect of a cubic building crowned by a central dome, or a group of domes, the middle one invariably being higher than the others. The uniformity of this architectural formula probably had a particular significance in contemporary eyes. Without being able to define its nature, we must remember that the Christian temple in the form of a cube with a central dome appears in the fifth century, in the little church of Christ Latomos in Thessalonica, and

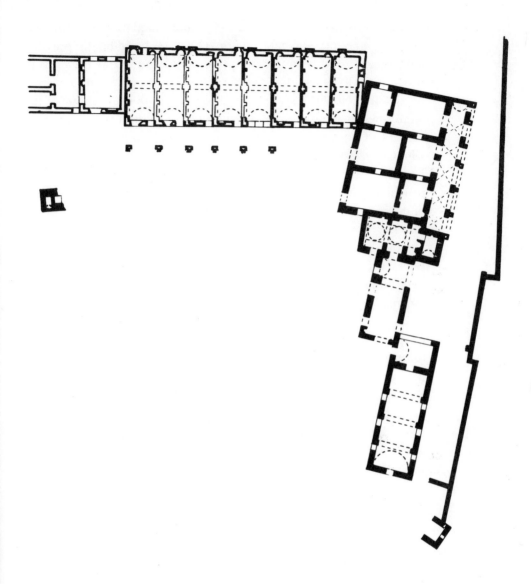

⊘ ⟍↗

⊢————⊣ 5 m.

7 – Palace of the Despots, Mistra

towards the end of the sixth century we find this plan in the cathedral of St. Sophia in the town of Edessa. The latter building disappeared long ago, but a surviving description in verse in Syriac leaves us in no doubt as to its essential characteristics. It was cubic and crowned by a dome. Now the same description claims that the shape of the church was an imitation on a reduced scale of the shape of the universe. In Constantinople, about 900 — that is to say, in the period when this type of church was definitely beginning to replace the basilica in Byzantium — the iconographic decoration and the way in which paintings were arranged on the vaults and interior walls of cubic churches definitely imply that the idea of an ecclesiastical building as microcosm was still in the minds of the Byzantines. It is possible that the consistency of these essential characteristics in the ecclesiastical buildings of the Middle Ages and the architects' determination invariably to give them the appearance of a cube crowned by a dome corresponds to this symbolism.

Historians of Byzantine architecture can distinguish between churches of different periods, between those of the ninth and the fourteenth centuries, but the characteristics which allow them to date these buildings approximately are details of the building or of the decoration, or even slight differences of style (the proportions are taller and slimmer, the barrels of the domes higher, the area inside larger, the brick ornaments on the façades increase as time advances, between the dates just mentioned). But all these indications are not very accurate: they can be misleading when monuments widely separated in time are compared. As always and everywhere, there were works by masters who invented something new and by artisans skilled in lightening the supports and walls, and others by builders who through incompetence and prudence tended towards massiveness and squatness, so that chronology does not really count. All the same at the beginning of the period considered we find in the provinces, for example on the island of Skyros and at Skripou in Boeotia (873–874), buildings that are particularly heavy and squat with very low drums and thick walls, whereas in the fourteenth and fifteenth centuries, in the capital of Morea, Mistra, the churches of the Peribleptos Virgin and the Pantanassa Virgin are graceful and elegant.

PLATE 29 – Mosaics in the apse at Monreale in Sicily, *ca.* 1148. *Cf. p. 149*

PLATE 30 – The Birth of Mary. Mosaic at Daphni near Athens, *ca.* 1100. *Cf. p. 140*

PLATE 31 – Mural paintings in the choir of St. Sophia at Ochrid, Macedonia (Yugoslavia), middle of XIth century. *Cf. p. 151*

PLATE 32 – The Burial of Christ. Mural painting at Nerez, Macedonia (Yugoslavia), 1164. *Cf. p. 152*

PLATE 33 – The Archangel of the Annunciation. Kurbinovo, Macedonia (Yugoslavia), end of xiith ▶ century. *Cf. p. 154*

PLATE 34 – St. Elizabeth fleeing with the infant St. John. Rock-cut chapel of St. Eustace in Cappadocia, beginning of xth century. *Cf. p. 157*

PLATE 35 — Miniature depicting Emperor Constantine the Great and St. Helena, his mother. XIth century. Palatine Library, Parma (Palatine manuscript 5).

PLATE 36 – Prayer in Gethsemane and Judas hanging. Miniature in a psalter, *ca.* 900. *Bibliothèque Nationale, Paris (MS. Grec 20). Cf. p. 167*

It is not this slight and barely perceptible evolution, but on the contrary the stability of architectural tradition which strikes one in Byzantium. Whereas during the same period in all the Western countries complex Carolingian churches, solid Romanesque sanctuaries, Gothic cathedrals and minsters succeed one another, with a whole range of distinct styles at each stage in the history of architecture, the Byzantines in no way modified the essential characteristics of their temples of worship, which from the ninth century onwards were established for all time.

To enumerate existing buildings, even limiting oneself to the most famous would appear to serve no purpose in a book such as this. But a few examples of churches deserve to be mentioned for one reason or another. These are in general quoted in chronological order, modified sometimes by topographical considerations, which from many points of view often have a greater effect on works of art than the actual date of their creation. MONUMENTS

So in Constantinople, apart from the churches of Basil I, only known through descriptions, we must note the church in the monastery of Constantine Lips (911). Today in ruins, and known by the Turkish name of Fener Isa Mejid, it was originally a superb work of architecture; in spite of its early date, it has fine proportions and astonishes one with the lightness of its interior supports and its large number of openings. This building shows the Byzantine architecture of about 900 making full use of its resources, already employing a complete vaulting which yet allowed numerous openings to be pierced in its walls. The Byzantine system of concentrating a number of thrusts of an arch on a limited number of points, where they are shouldered, allows the lightening of other parts of the masonry, including the insertion of a great number of openings. In this church, and most others in Constantinople and Thessalonica, openings of this type in the lateral walls of the church give on to outdoor galleries. These were destroyed in Istanbul in Turkish times. But fine examples are still to be found in St. Catherine and in the Holy Apostles in Thessalonica. CONSTANTI-NOPLE

Fener Isa

PLAN I, P. 103

Still in Istanbul, in the middle of the tenth century a church dedicated to the Saviour was built with a crypt in which Emperor Romanus I, the Lecapenus (920–944), was buried. This very fine *Myrelaion* building, today in ruins, is remarkable for the harmony of its proportions. One can see in this church, which is also called the Myrelaion, a fine example of a system of vaults; these surround the central dome and, in order better to support it, buttress it symmetrically at the base of the barrel by four cradle vaults, each joined to one exterior wall of the church. These four vaults together form the arms of a more or less symmetrical cross, which is the reason why buildings of this type are called churches with a cross within a square or rectangle.

Churches of the Pantocrator

There are other churches in Constantinople of this same type, naturally with differences in detail. We may note in particular the group of two churches in the ancient monastery of the Pantocrator (Turkish name: Zeirek Camii), built in a straight line and joined by a vestibule. This is a double sanctuary, with a chapel between the two churches which was used as a mausoleum by the emperors of the Comnenus family. In Constantinople it is the only important example of architecture of the Comnenian period. Two centuries separate the churches of the Pantocrator from that of Constantine Lips. But the only difference between this and the churches founded by the Comneni is in points of detail.

Churches of the Virgin Pammacharistos and of Christ in Chora

Two more centuries separate the churches of the Pantocrator and the sanctuaries built and reconstructed by the Palaeologi or their contemporaries, such as the church of the Virgin Pammacharistos (Fetie Camii), that of Christ in Chora (Kariye Camii) or the south church of the monastery of Constantine Lips (Fener Isa). But once again the evolution of the ecclesiastical building is barely perceptible. It is practically the same, although the nave of the Chora and of Lips are not of the usual architectural type. In neither do four arms of a cross spring from the dome to join the outer walls, but in the south church of the monastery of Lips an angled corridor supports the dome on three sides, and in the Chora the domed chamber is devoid of all collaterals. However, there is no question here of innovations, but only a return to architectural forms known since the pre-Iconoclast period. As in the examples mentioned above, the Byzantine architects of the Middle Ages revived plans and types of elevation they found in ancient monuments. But it was practically obligatory for the exterior of all these buildings, including precisely the churches of the Chora and Fener Isa (southern church), to come back to the cube crowned by a dome.

On the other hand what is most typical is that numerous edifices of the thirteenth and fourteenth centuries in Constantinople were built on to older sanctuaries, often reconstructed for this purpose. This is exactly the case with regard to the two sanctuaries we have just mentioned: at Fener Isa a second church and a vast double vestibule have been added to a building of the tenth century, whereas in the Chora an older restored church is completed by two narthex and side buildings, one of which is a fine south chapel. It is probable that the threatening political situation in Constantinople during this period was unfavourable to the building of completely new sanctuaries. Whereas the medieval Byzantine churches in Istanbul are generally in a lamentable state, those in Thessalonica are carefully looked after and often restored, and give us an excellent idea of the architecture of medieval urban churches.

In Thessalonica nearly all the surviving churches date from the fourteenth century, a period of prosperity in this great city. Unlike the buildings in Constantinople of that period, those in Mistra and Thessalonica were new foundations. They belong entirely to the architecture of the Palaeologi. The series of these medieval sanctuaries begins with a church dedicated to the Virgin of the Metal-Workers, ('tôn Chalkéôn'), built in 1028. But more interesting are St. Catherine (about 1300), the Holy Apostles (1312–1315) and St. Panteleimon (fourteenth century), where the body of the cubic edifice is, or was formerly, surrounded on three 'sides by a corridor or gallery. We have had a glimpse of this in several churches of the same period in Constantinople; but there it is only suggested, because of the state of preservation of the churches, whereas in Thessalonica we can see it entirely preserved in at least two churches. The method of conceiving these galleries and detaching them from the central core varies from one monument to the other. But the architects quite obviously sought to make use of this surrounding gallery. The version found in St. Catherine and the Holy Apostles tends to make these galleries, when seen from the outside, an integral part of the central building. On these galleries are placed four secondary domes, which with their roofs look like a series of pyramids.

Churches of Thessalonica

PLAN 5, P. 107

The galleries of St. Panteleimon were lighter and opened up by colonnades. In the Taxiarchs, a small church built on different levels, they are covered in wood, except at the eastern end, where these galleries are blocked by little chapels.

Church of St. Elias The church of St. Elias in Thessalonica deserves special mention. It is a monastery church built on a three-apse plan, and has in front a spacious entrance hall, such as is often found on Mount Athos. Specialists in the archaeology of Thessalonica have sought to date this imposing building to the middle of the fourteenth century. If this is correct, then the severe grandeur of this massive structure and the shape of the barrel with its flat niches and horizontal cornice must be explained by the influence of earlier buildings.

PLATE P. 90 Whereas there were simultaneously old time-honoured sanctuaries (the cathedral of St. Sophia, St. Demetrius, the Acheiropoetos Virgin) and a host of small medieval churches in use in the city of Thessalonica during the Middle Ages, the situation in Athens was

Churches of Athens somewhat different. The Parthenon, transformed by several interior alterations, was the great shrine of the Virgin. Flanked by a chapel installed in the Erechtheon, the Christian Parthenon dominated the large number of small churches in the lower town dating from the eleventh to the fourteenth century, which still exist.

PLAN 4, P. 106 In Athens the oldest and finest medieval churches are from the eleventh century: the churches of the Apostles, of the Saviour Lykodimou, of St. Theodore, and of the Kapnikarea. Although the architecture of the interior differs as far as the central dome and its supports are concerned (pendentives and four supports or squinches and eight supports), each of these churches, viewed from the outside, is a cube covered by a system of roofs, the largest of which form the arms of a cross upon which rests the barrel of the dome. Their façades, devoid of all plastic decoration, have rows of bricks running around them at different heights. Around the windows, on the walls and barrels, brick arches enliven the walls, built in carefully cut stone. Lastly, bricks and tiles embedded in mortar are used to make occasional ornaments imitating ancient Arabic inscriptions. These are frequent but generally isolated reflections of contemporary Muslim architecture.

The churches in Athens are without side galleries, except for the

Kapnikarea, which was later completed (in the fourteenth century?) by a chapel and an arcaded entrance hall connected to the church proper. An especial exception is the church at Daphni, which has its PLAN 3, P. 105 raised entrance hall, the latter starting with an elegant arcade in the classical style, emphasized by fluted columns copied from a monument on the Acropolis. We will merely mention the charming little church of 'the old Metropolis', a work which might be of the APPX. PL. 4 twelfth century and not of the tenth as used to be thought. The interest of this little building lies not in its commonplace architecture, but in the very original reliefs that cover its façade.

As in Athens, the finest monastic churches of the district are of the eleventh century, the sanctuaries of Daphni and of Hosios (the Blessed) Lucas being the main ones. Both are built near classical pagan holy places, Eleusis and Delphi, though their origins have no connection. The church of Daphni is smaller and more slender and APPX. PL. 6
APPX. PL. 5, 10 bathed in light; that of Hosios Lucas larger and heavier, littered with galleries, complicated by special interior arrangements to surround the tomb of its founder. Both have a common characteristic: large domes on a squat barrel, supported by squinches and eight pillars. This type of dome, which allowed space that might be used for a larger chamber — the diameter of domes on pendentives being generally smaller — was much admired in Greece in the eleventh century. In addition to the two churches we have just mentioned, there are also another church with mosaics, that on the island of Chios, St. Sophia in Monemvasia, Christianou in Trephilia, St. Theodore in Mistra and lastly the church of Christ Lykodimou in Athens itself, already mentioned. In Constantinople and Salonika none of the known sanctuaries have the same kind of construction, but this is probably the result of destruction, as at Preslav, the Bulgarian capital, where art was inspired by that of Constantinople. The church at the place known as Patleina has a dome on squinches and a plan similar to that in the churches of the Daphni type.

In Attica and in all the central provinces of Greece, as well as in the coastal regions of the Peloponnese, Byzantine religious architecture is poorly represented by monuments of the late Middle Ages. This whole area was then in the hands of the Franks and Catalans, or even of the Venetians, so that the finest and oldest churches, as for example Daphni, were reserved for Roman worship. The Greeks no longer founded new churches there and were content to carry out alterations — as at the Kapnikarea in Athens, where the great entrance hall of original appearance was probably added to in the fourteenth century.

On the other hand, Greek cities that the dismemberment of the empire in the thirteenth and fourteenth centuries raised to the rank of little political capitals, such as Mistra near Sparta and Arta in Epirus, only possessed churches of the Palaeologian period. Their number is even surprising, but given the traditional small size of ecclesiastical buildings in this period (the reduced scale of churches tended to become even more marked), one is led to believe that each sanctuary had its own liturgical use. But the prestige of founding a sanctuary must also have played its part, in that the princelings of Morea and Epirus felt obliged to follow the example of the powerful emperors of the past in this respect.

Churches of Mistra At Mistra, the church of St. Sophia (middle of the fourteenth century) and various chapels are attached to the Palace of the Despots. Of the other churches one called the Metropolis of St. Demetrius served as a cathedral; the remainder, all situated on the periphery of the town, belonged to monasteries. These included

APPX. PL. 9 St. Theodore (1290–1295) and the sanctuaries of the Virgin: Hodigitria, also called Brontocheion or Aphentiko (1311–1312), Peribleptos (fourteenth century) and Pantanassa (1428). Founded shortly before 1300 as a basilica with three naves and a narthex, the church of the Metropolis was transformed in the fifteenth century into a church in the form of an inscribed cross with five domes, this conception having been borrowed from the churches of the fourteenth century in Mistra. Two of these churches in particular might have served as models: the Hodigitria and the Pantanassa where one already finds the basilica plan (a large and short basilica, three naves united together forming a square, and only three columns in each row); the roofs are dominated by a central dome, around which are grouped smaller and lower domes. The Hodigitria has galleries that stretch as far as the apsidioles. In these two churches the secondary domes are blind calottes without barrels, whereas other premises, some built on to the side of the church and others added in front of the façade, are also vaulted with blind calottes. The first of these churches has its narthex prolonged laterally from the two sides. But as later on in the Metropolis, of all these secondary vaults there are four which emerge in the form of small barrels, blind or with windows, in such a way that when viewed from the outside each of these churches looks like a cubic edifice with a system of roofs dominated by the conventional group of five domes and roofs in the form of a cross. The beautiful churches of Mistra afford the most characteristic examples of this method, typically Byzantine, of differentiating between the interior construction and the exterior aspect as defined by the roofing. All this brings us back, as always in such cases, to the statement that the Byzantines attached special importance to the external appearance of religious buildings. On this point the Palaeologian period remained faithful to the practice of earlier centuries.

This faithfulness to the architectural practices of the past is just as PLAN 6, P. 108 apparent in the plans and construction of the other churches of Mistra: St. Theodore, with its large dome on squinches and eight supports, St. Sophia, the Peribleptos and the Evangelisatria, which are churches on the classical plan: a dome on pendentives and four supports. In fact, instead of four pillars or four columns, the architects chose furthermore to have the dome small, supported on two pillars (the ends of the separating walls between the three compartments of the choir) and two columns. This system had the advantage of opening up the area reserved for the faithful. The repetition of the same design in three different churches, like the repetition in three other churches of the idea of the five domes on a basilica, points to the use of the same workshops. The enthusiasm of the founders of the churches and the palace at Mistra grew for over a century, and local workmen did not have to look for work elsewhere; that is why the ruins of this town offer such a fine field for the study of late Byzantine architecture. Thus it is easier here to observe the different forms of art practised by one workshop, its relative richness and its limitation, its attachment to the past and what is produced that was original.

In the fourteenth century this workshop at Mistra did not contradict the architecture of the Palaeologian period that we spoke of above, referring to the monuments in Constantinople and Thessalonica. It has already been noted that, as in the latter city, the churches of the fourteenth century at Mistra are entirely new and not additions to earlier buildings, as in the Byzantine capital. But in the majority of cases, and particularly when it was a question of monastic churches, at Mistra one sees what has already been noted in the eleventh-century buildings at Constantinople: the main body of the church is completed by new rings, various vestibules, chapels or mausoleums, refectories and other rooms built on to the walls of the church, and sometimes, as at Peribleptos, to the side of the apses.

Search for the picturesque

This occasionally produces the aspect of a mass of dissimilar buildings, but also of picturesque architectural groups which are beautiful to look at. According to some critics the quest for the picturesque was one of the main preoccupations of the builders of the Palaeologian period. This conclusion is inaccurate, whether one takes it generally or limits it solely to the Palaeologian era. However, all the monasteries around Mistra show interesting examples of this. In some cases the picturesque groups of various buildings are dominated by a church tower. Earlier Byzantine architecture seems not to have known the use of a church belfry in the form of a tower with storeys of lattice-work. This was probably borrowed from Western art during the domination of the Franks. We must add an example from the thirteenth century at Stanimachus and another from the fourteenth at Mesembria (see below) to the examples at Mistra of St. Sophia, the Hodigitria and the Pantanassa. Towers in the form of walls pierced by arcades, as at the Metropolis at Mistra, probably have the same Western origin. The quest for the picturesque is emphasized by the effects of bichromate on the façades (red brick, stone and rough-cast ornamental motifs in bricks of different shapes) common to the majority of Byzantine buildings of the Middle Ages, but which on the façades of the Palaeologian period were remarkable. Among the few innovations were the festoons in brick crowned with rosettes that decorate the apses of the Pantanassa and appear to imitate the decoration of the apses at Monreale (twelfth century) near Palermo. Apart from these few particularities, the architecture of Mistra, which belongs entirely to the art of the Palaeologi, is a child of the monumental art of Constantinople.

During the thirteenth century a Greek state known as the despotate of Epirus came into being in north-western Greece, governed by the Ducas. These princes filled their capital, Arta, with churches, many of which are still standing. Like the cathedral, dedicated to the Virgin Parigoritissa (about 1290), nearly all these churches date from the thirteenth century: St. Demetrius (built in the tenth century, re-built in the thirteenth), the Virgin Kato-Panagia, the Virgin of the Blachernes (outside the town), St. Basil and St. APPX. PL. 2 Theodora.

Coming from Mistra to Arta one immediately feels the difference; at Arta everything is more provincial and nearly always more rustic. The art practised there was less pure, for two distinct reasons: less skilful workmanship and foreign infiltrations into Byzantine architecture. It was also more conservative, even archaist. The Parigoritissa, from the thirteenth century, imitates a APPX. PL. 7 massive cube, like that of Hosios Lucas in Phocis, at least two centuries earlier. As in this older church, the dome rests on squinches. But this architectural form is no longer understood at Arta where, probably under Gothic influence, the niches of the squinches are flanked by four rows of thin little columns one above the other. As the roofs are reduced to a single horizontal line one loses the advantage of the undulations of the roofing which are an attraction in so many Byzantine churches. Other churches are in the form of basilicas, having short wide naves with slender supports (either columns alone or alternating with pillars). Some, like the Kato-Panagia, have a narrow transept in front of the choir; others, like St. Demetrius, were re-built in the thirteenth century, in order to replace the wooden roofs by a system of vaults with a central dome, the essential characteristic roof for churches in the shape of an inscribed cross and central dome. Several of these churches and in particular St. Basil are richly decorated with ornamental bricks on all their façades, especially on the exterior wall of the chevet, in a manner very akin to that found on twelfth-century Norman churches in Sicily.

All the architecture of Arta is very alike. The same art is also characteristic of the thirteenth- to fourteenth-century churches at Kastoria (in western Macedonia), Porta Panagia in Thessaly,

Trikkala and generally in the western half of northern Greece as far as the lakes of Macedonia. One feature common to all churches of this area, which also stretches northwards into the region of what is now Yugoslav Macedonia (for example Štip, Prilep, Monastir), is their archaism. They still kept to basilicas even in the middle of the Palaeologian era; the supports between the nave and the collaterals were of a simple type or of two alternating types. The basilica could either have a transept or not; it could have a wooden roof or vaults. It was in the thirteenth century that the wooden roof was replaced by the vaults and a central dome, a change which in Constantinople had been carried out in basilicas from the Justinian period onwards. We have explained above how in many towns of northern Greece in the Middle Ages the cathedral kept to its basilical architecture and how it went back to the paleo-Christian era or was re-built in mid-medieval times on the antique model, as at Serres, Trikkala and Mesembria. In north-western Greece this attachment to archaic forms spreads to all churches. This, one imagines, is due not only to their distance from Constantinople and Thessalonica, but also to the strength of local paleo-Christian tradition. In this region, which at the time of the despotate of Epirus had better communications with Italy, the north of Albania and Serbia than with Byzantium, paleo-Christian traditions were easily joined to those of Latin inspiration. On the other hand in Greek Macedonia, even when it was in the hands of Bulgars and Serbs, and as far as the town of Mesembria on the Black Sea, religious architecture, at least after the eleventh century, followed Thessalonica and Constantinople. The surviving churches in Bulgaria which go back to the conversion of the Bulgars (843) and to the period immediately after are basilicas and rotundas — that is to say, they are buildings which revive the paleo-Christian tradition (Preslav, Pliska, the 'martyrium' of Ochrid and Prespa). On the other hand, the builders of the later churches of the Patleina in Preslav, of St. Sophia in Ochrid (before 1050) and all the medieval ecclesiastical architects in the northern and north-eastern Balkans, whatever the ruling political régime or the nationality of their craftsmen, allowed themselves to be guided by the art in vogue in Constantinople and Thessalonica. Thus it now seems to have been proved that the

Churches of north-eastern Greece

APPX. PL. I

Religious architecture in Greek Macedonia

cathedral of St. Sophia in Ochrid was built after the Byzantine re-conquest of Bulgaria; it follows the style of a cubic church with a dome, with an inscribed cross. This type of building, with variations in its secondary features, is found again in 1164 at Nerez near Skoplje and in 1295 at Ochrid in the church of the Peribleptos Virgin, later called St. Clement, as also in those founded by the Serbian princes in Macedonia in the fourteenth century. The latter are directly related in their architecture to the Palaeologian church-es at Lesnovo, Gračanica and elsewhere. This same art reached the Greek cities on the western shores of the Black Sea, such as Mesem-bria, today Nesebar in Bulgaria. This little town until lately still *Mesembria* wore its medieval aspect, and all its churches present us with a characteristic collection of sanctuaries: a huge basilica in ruins, rightly attributed to the ninth century, a church of the twelfth–thirteenth centuries, in the form of a basilica but smaller, and about ten later churches, five or six of which go back to the fourteenth century: the Pantocrator, the Archangels, the two churches of St. John, St. Paraskevi and St. Theodore. They are mostly fine examples of the Palaeologian type of cubic building in the form of an in-scribed cross and central dome. The Pantocrator and the Arch-angels have a tower, as at Mistra. Everywhere the façades are elegantly decorated with niches, the red of the bricks alternating with the bright colour of the cut stone. Minute reliefs, rows of discs and rosettes in green glazed ceramic complete this decor. Three churches at Mesembria — St. John-Aliturgitos, the Pantocrator and the Archangels are as fine as the best ecclesiastical architecture of the fourteenth century in Thessalonica and Mistra. The town of Mesembria must have experienced a period of great prosperity in the fourteenth century, following a less favourable one, to have been able to add so many artistic sanctuaries to the two earlier churches. The ceramic sculptured façades of the thirteenth and fourteenth *Ceramic sculptured* centuries have not yet been sufficiently studied for us to determine *façades of XIIIth and* their origin. The question depends above all on that of the possible *XIVth centuries* influence of Seljuk architecture in Persia, where from the tenth century one can see remarkable examples of decoration by the use of bricks in suitable designs. But in the West as well in the Roman-esque period similar methods of decoration in brick were known.

The examples to be seen in Sicily have a particularly clear relationship to Byzantine buildings. Another question arises about this decoration: was it first used in churches or in lay buildings?

SECULAR
ARCHITECTURE
It has been said earlier that few monuments of Byzantine architecture other than religious buildings remain. We must add that, unlike many other artists elsewhere, those of Byzantium in the Middle Ages did not represent actual secular buildings in painting or sculpture; Byzantine writers rarely describe them and then only *Palaces of the emperors* incompletely. It is the same with the Imperial Palace at Con-*at Constantinople* stantinople, where generation after generation of sovereigns built and transformed the various main buildings, which comprised their apartments and reception rooms. The little information that one can derive from texts on the subject does not allow one to reconstruct them even approximately; and all that one can gather, which is by no means uninteresting, is that, whereas the Imperial Palace at Constantinople in ancient times consisted essentially of courtyards with porches and basilica-like rooms, the new palaces of the time of the Iconoclasts and Macedonians consisted of state rooms in the middle, with niches and vaulted domes. No technical knowledge about the palaces built in the twelfth century under the Comneni has come down to us. These palaces had the peculiarity of being more closely linked than was the great antique palace before to churches, such as that of the Blachernes or that of the Forty Martyrs.

We know that these palaces had a first floor on which the most important rooms were situated. Miniatures in the Chronicles of the Skylitzes in the National Library in Madrid (thirteenth and fourteenth centuries) confirm this. These rooms on the piano nobile, supported by arcades, were the historic setting in which many events in the Imperial Palace took place. According to these same miniatures another characteristic of these palaces was that this storey overhung the ground floor, in the same way as they did in the more modern baronial mansions in towns throughout the Balkans. This custom was usual everywhere in the Mediterranean.

Only one Byzantine palace in Constantinople remains, situated not far from the Blachernes. Known by its Turkish name of Tekfur *Tekfur Serai* Serai, it has been attributed to various periods. But the decoration of its façade in ceramic sculpture leaves no doubt that this building was of the same period as the Palaeologian churches. It has a rectangular main portion with two rows of windows, one above the APPX. PL. 14 other, and inside it are traces of two superimposed storeys. The façade is well-proportioned and elegant.

Another palace and a certain number of baronial mansions, in ruins, remain at Mistra; M. Orlandos and others have attempted *Palaces and baronial mansions at Mistra* reconstructions which appear satisfactory. The Palace of the Despots of Morea has a number of main buildings, the most important of which have at least two storeys of chambers and rooms, some of the windows of each storey giving out on to one of the long walls and others on to the corridor or terrace that ran along the other wall. The exterior aspect of this building greatly resembles that of the tribunal of Pomposa, near Venice, and contemporary Venetian palaces. The surrounds of the windows of the main storey in the palace at Mistra APPX. PL. 13 are Gothic, and this accentuates the likeness. It is quite probable in fact that baronial architecture of the Palaeologian period was influenced by Italian and Frankish secular art. As we shall see, in the painting, and partly in the plastic and decorative arts, of the Palaeologi, religious and secular art can be distinguished by the fact that ecclesiastical art was closely tied to the Orthodox religion of the Greeks and was for them almost a national tradition, whereas the secular art cultivated by the princes and lords was at the same time more personal, more transitory, as a result more easily affected by passing fashions, whatever their origin.

IV. PAINTING, SCULPTURE AND THE ORNAMENTAL ARTS FROM THE END OF ICONOCLASM TO THE SACK OF CONSTANTINOPLE BY THE CRUSADERS IN 1204

MOSAICS   During this period it was in parietal mosaics that the Byzantines created their most remarkable works. This form of art, which reached technical perfection in the first centuries of our era, underwent a revival from the fourth century onwards, particularly in the important Christian sanctuaries of the period. The mosaic decoration of the domes and vaults of St. Sophia and other sanctuaries built by Justinian in the middle of the sixth century, remained in the same tradition. On the other hand, the mosaics of St. Apollinare Nuovo in Ravenna and a few other monuments of the period heralded the medieval practice of lining the walls of churches with mosaics, whose predominating theme was no longer merely decorative but Christian iconography.

In theory the art of iconographical mosaics should have reappeared in 843, immediately after the victory over Iconoclasm. But it appears rather that, judging from the early works at least, a more active revival of sacred imagery in the churches can only have taken place one or two decades after this date. Two works of that period have been preserved: a famous mosaic which occupies a tympanum over the main entrance of St. Sophia and another which decorates the calotte of the dome of St. Sophia in Salonika. The latter has as its main subject Christ Enthroned in Majesty, at his feet a kneeling emperor, while in two symmetrical medallions appear busts of the Virgin and of an angel. The composition most probably represents Christ in all his Wisdom, patron of the cathedral of Constantinople, the two side figures evoking the Annunciation, that is to say the beginning of the Incarnation and consequently the work of Salvation accomplished by Divine Wisdom. The emperor is Leo VI, the Wise (886–912). This mosaic is solemn and a little heavy. All that the Byzantine artists did here was to take up again a tradition of figurative art that had been interrupted for a long time.

The same impression is produced by the contemporary mosaic at

St. Sophia in Thessalonica. This is a vast composition of the PLATE P. 90
Ascension, remarkable for the play of colours and golds and for the
expression on some of the faces — Mary, the angels and some apostles, but the clumsiness of the mosaicists is also obvious. One has only
to observe the way in which they render the rapid movements of
the figures and the lack of proportion between these figures and the
central motif of Christ in all His Glory. The latter is too small
because the artists had no experience of images spread out on a
concave surface.

Similar circumstances are probably responsible for the lack of *Mosaics of St. Sophia*
stability, rare in Byzantine mosaics, of the figure of the Virgin *in Constantinople*
Enthroned with Child on the vault of the apse of St. Sophia in
Constantinople. Archaeologists entirely disagree as to the date of
this remarkable work (ascribing it to the ninth, eleventh and fourteenth centuries). Personally I tend towards the earlier date and
link this image of the Virgin as well as the two angels on either side
of her (of which only one survives) with the small group of mosaics
executed shortly after the fall of the Iconoclasts. Whatever the date,
the art of this mosaic and more particularly the strange beauty of
the heads of Mary and the Angel show the presence of a great artist.
In St. Sophia the entire surface available for decoration in this colossal building does not seem to have been covered with mosaics. In
the tenth century, however, several remarkable mosaics, entirely
independent of each other and of different dates, were placed there.
Only recently we have been able to admire a fine portrait of Emperor Alexander, who reigned for less than two years after the death
of his brother Leo VI (912). An imperial couple dating from a
century later, finished around 1042, represents Constantine Monomachus and Zoe. Another panel with John Comnenus and Irene
(around 1118–1122) accompanied by their son Alexius is a later
form of art, but also belongs to the same category of votive imperial
portraits. Returning to the tenth century, we must also note in the
cathedral of St. Sophia two groups of mosaics of very high quality.
First of all, in the south vestibule, a Mary with Child receiving from
the Emperor Constantine the offering of the city he had founded
and which bore his name and from the Emperor Justinian a gift
of the church of St. Sophia which he had rebuilt. The other series

of mosaics high up on the lateral walls of the nave show large figures treated as portraits (or considered as such) of the Prophets and the Patriarchs of Constantinople. These are admirable pictures in which the classical taste and knowledge of the period are evident from the way in which the draped figures and faces are constructed, so that one feels the plastic volume and structure; the facial features of each of the Patriarchs clearly show them as individuals. One of these portraits, that of the eunuch Ignatius, is powerful and realistic and was certainly painted from life. We would not be mistaken in thinking that this interest in realistic portraits which were likenesses was also a result of classical studies. This was the starting point for an attempt to give the appearance of a portrait with individual features to the image of St. John Chrysostom which figures amongst the mosaics of the Patriarchs. These same personages, who lived in the fourth and fifth centuries, when shown in earlier mosaics did not have such an individual appearance.

Mosaic decorations of Hosios Lucas

Chronologically the mosaics that are most like those in St. Sophia are to be found far from the Byzantine capital, in continental Greece. In the latter case we are dealing with a mosaic decoration which originally covered all vaults and arches of a monastic church. This sanctuary, built in the mountains of Phocis, not far from Delphi, is dedicated to a local anchorite, the Blessed Lucas, and surrounds his tomb. The mosaics were made there shortly after the year 1000 by craftsmen of whose origin we know nothing. Their art is far removed from that of the mosaicists of St. Sophia. In particular we are far from all that in St. Sophia recalled Hellenic art, including the subtle colouring of the works which originated in the capital. It is a harder and more graphic form of art; shapes are simple, proportions squat, expressions sad or serious, movement absent or rare, though abrupt. All these features make one think of a provincial art verging on folklore. This may be a correct impression, but it could be deceptive: owing to the distance which separates us in time, it is generally impossible to be sure. One thing is certain, that this work from the beginning of the eleventh century seems to have recaptured none of the influences of the tenth-century 'renaissance'. From the point of view of shape they could have been derived from mosaics of the type of those in St. Sophia in Salonika, executed at

PLATE 37 – Moses receiving the Law on Mount Sinai. Miniature. *Vatican Library (Reg. Suev. Gr. 1).* *Cf. p. 169*

135

PLATE 38 – The Prophet Nathan: detail of the scene of David's Repentance. xth-century miniature from a psalter. *Bibliothèque Nationale, Paris (MS. Grec 139)*. *Cf. p. 169*

PLATE 39 – The Seven Sleepers of Ephesus. Miniature in a menology (calendar) belonging to the Emperor Basil II, *ca.* 1000. *Vatican Library (Cod. Gr. 1613)*. *Cf. p. 171*

PLATE 40 – The Crucifixion and the Dividing of Christ's Garments. Miniature in a book of the Gospels, middle of xith century. *Bibliothèque Nationale, Paris (MS. Grec 74). Cf. pp. 174, 175*

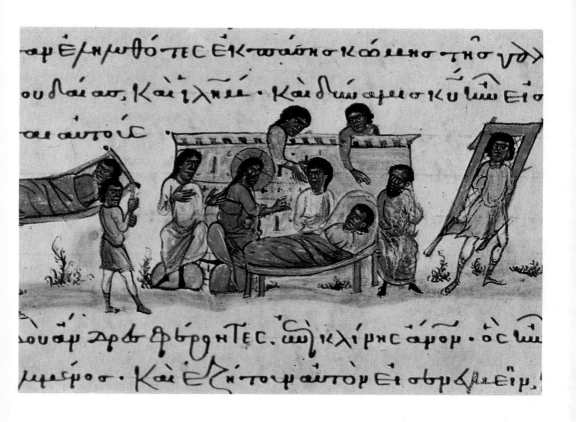

PLATE 41 – The Healing of the Man Sick of the Palsy. xiith-century miniature in the Gospel. *Laurentian Library, Florence (VI. 23). Cf. p. 175*

PLATE 42 – The Denial of St. Peter. Miniature in a book of Gospels, XIIth century. *Palatine Library,* *Parma (Cod. 5). Cf. p. 176*

PLATE 43 – Painted ornamental decoration in a book of Gospels, *ca.* 1100. *Bibliothèque Nationale, Paris.*

PLATE 44 – Child (?) and bear eating honey. Death of St. Basil. xiith-century paintings. *Bibliothèque Nationale, Paris (MS. Grec 550). Cf. p. 179*

the end of the ninth century. The art of Hosios Lucas can also in part be compared to the mural paintings of the tenth century in central Italy, which in turn may have reflected slightly earlier Byzantine works (a church set up in the temple of Fortune Virile in Rome; Cimitile). As to the scheme of the Hosios Lucas paintings, they follow a model which seems to have been evolved in Constantinople around 900 and to have been designed more particularly for the decoration of cubic churches with a central dome (see above on architecture). The dome of Hosios Lucas is occupied by a figure of Christ Pantocrator. Below were placed the Archangels, the Virgin, John the Baptist and the Prophets, who have today disappeared; on the large pendentives which supported the dome the first events of the Gospel were commemorated by important liturgical feasts — the Annunciation, the Nativity, the Purification and the Baptism. PLATE P. 93 In the conch of the apse there is a large figure of the Virgin Enthroned with Child and in front of the calotte a famous Pentecost in which we see the Holy Ghost descending on the Apostles seated in a circle and below, in the pendentives, the people gathering around the Pentecostal Table. Apart from these few scenes, we find in the nave and in the choir with its dependencies merely portraits of Saints of all categories, among them many Bishops, Apostles and Martyrs. The most curious of these effigies are portraits of local monastic saints and particularly of the founder of the convent, Hosios Lucas, who came from the neighbouring village of Stiris.

The vestibule provides a final cycle of panels in mosaic among which are two rather crude pictures of the Washing of the Feet and the Unbelief of Thomas and two excellent compositions which face one on entering the church; a Crucifixion and a Descent into Limbo. Through the splendid balance of the masses and the power of expression these two scenes are among the most remarkable in the church. Also in the vestibule there is an image of Christ with the same qualities of strength, but of a depressing hardness.

The art of the two other eleventh-century mosaic compositions that have been preserved in Greece cannot be considered as being derived from Hosios Lucas, and one has no connection with the other. However, the three works are related from certain points of view, particularly in regard to their iconographical scheme and the general principles of the presentation of the mosaics and of Christian subjects treated in mosaics.

Decoration of church of 'New Monastery' on Chios
Chronologically, the decoration of the church of the New Monastery on the island of Chios comes after that of Hosios Lucas. According to a tradition it was the Emperor Constantine Monomachus (1042–1054) who ordered these mosaics, and this is not contradicted by an examination of the mosaics we find there. There does indeed exist a certain resemblance between the style of these mosaics and that of the miniatures painted in 1066, in the Constantinople convent of Stoudion (illustrations of a Psalter at present in the British Museum, Add. MS. 19.352), and several other monuments of the same school, for example the Tetraevangile Paris MS. Grec 74. As in these paintings for the illustration of manuscripts, so also in the Chios mosaics we find scenes with more graceful and less heavy figures than those of Hosios Lucas. They have narrow sloping shoulders and ascetic elongated faces; their hair and their beards are black; their large piercing eyes beneath frowning eyebrows which join each other, give these personages an Oriental look. In the scenes one feels a taste for greater dramatic tension, whereas the portraits, however conventional, have a very individual appearance. The Hosios Lucas portraits are flat and graphic and impress one by their stiff rigidity; those of Chios are modelled and in consequence produce a different impression, while accentuating the structure of faces emaciated through fasting and vigils. It is perhaps here that the ascetic ideal of the Orthodox monk finds its first outstanding expression.

The subjects and the way in which they are distributed are very similar to those at Hosios Lucas. The simpler architecture of the church on Chios resulted in a more abbreviated iconographic scheme. The dome is filled by the Pantocrator surrounded by celestial forces, followed by Apostles and Evangelists; in the apse Mary rises praying, escorted by two Archangels, in two apsidioles behind; scenes from the Gospels are distributed over the pendentives, the four niches between them, and the narthex. The number of these scenes hardly exceeds the time-honoured figure of twelve, which is that of the main liturgical feasts. Here again, as in Hosios Lucas, the evangelical cycle corresponds essentially to that of the feasts.

Finally, on Chios, too, as we have seen, a portrait gallery of the Saints, but a smaller one, completes the collection of holy images. The third and last of the important mosaic decorations in Greece *Mosaics at Daphni* is at a place called Daphni, a few steps from Athens on the Eleusis road. As is the case with the other two, we know nothing about either their date or their origin. Once more the quality of the work makes one think of the mosaicists of Constantinople, but there is nothing to back up this hypothesis, as there is for the mosaics on Chios. It would in fact be difficult to quote another example of Byzantine painting in the same style as that of Daphni. We can, however, without too much difficulty find the theoretical place occupied by Daphni in the history of Byzantine painting thanks to the stylistic similarities between various details: the face of Christ; the other faces with their aquiline noses; the draperies and naked bodies modelled with a remarkable feeling for shape; the proportion of the faces; and the agreeable elegance of the figures and movements, even of whole compositions. All these features define an art which with less assurance appears in the mosaics of St. Sophia in Kiev, dated around 1040; in the twelfth century this was to be generally used in all the Byzantine countries and those under their influence. At Daphni we discover this future style of the Comnenian period in the second stage of its formation. So it is reasonable to date the mosaics of Daphni to the end of the eleventh century, as suggested by G. Millet.

In this connection one remark is necessary to give an idea of the way in which styles developed in Byzantium. The Daphni mosaics are much more Greek in feeling than any of the others. This proves a greater familiarity with the ancient Greek models than is evident in the other two mosaics preserved in Greece. On the other hand, the end of the eleventh century in Byzantium was not a period of a 'new renaissance' succeeding that of the tenth century. It was far more a period of stagnation and perhaps one when ideas were borrowed from the Islamic arts. In other words, the Daphni mosaics represent a particular trend in Byzantine art of the eleventh century, of which, apart from Daphni, our only knowledge comes from works produced later, during the Comnenian period (for example, the Sicilian mosaics of that period at Cefalù, at Martorana and the

Palatine Chapel in Palermo). Were it not for these later works, one might consider the possibility of the sculptors of the Parthenon having exercised a direct influence on the mosaicists of Daphni. After all this there is no reason to exclude the theory that in Athens and elsewhere the pleasant Hellenic style, with its sinuous lines and graceful rhythms, evolved after more systematic study of classical reliefs. If all the mosaics of that period, with their backgrounds and their figures draped in light garments, predominantly in white, remind one of delicately coloured bas-reliefs, the graceful classical style of Daphni makes this comparison a particularly happy one (cf. above, on the porch at Daphni).

There are many gaps in the decoration of Daphni. That which remains shows us an iconographic scheme and a way of organizing the subjects similar to that used at Hosios Lucas and Chios. The Daphni Pantocrator is in the dome in its usual place. But its Oriental and particularly severe type is astonishing when compared with the other graceful Hellenic mosaics. The artists must have reproduced an earlier Christ. Beneath the Pantocrator, in the barrel, we again find the row of Prophets and in the apse the Theotokos, which in the chevet of the church is accompanied by two archangels, St. John the Baptist and several personages who evoke the sacrifice of the Eucharist. Other saints are portrayed on the walls of the nave. But one of the innovations at Daphni is the extension of the cycle of scenes which here occupy the corner squinches, and also the higher part of the walls of the nave, as well as certain places in the narthex. In the nave alone there were originally thirteen evangelical scenes, which followed the chronological order of events as is usual in cycles of frescoes. The choice of subjects starts off with the same cycle of important feasts, but one strays further afield than at Hosios Lucas or Chios, and the evangelical scenes of the nave in particular are completed by two series of subjects taken from the Passion of our PLATE P. 112 Lord and from the Childhood of the Virgin, which are in the narthex: the Last Supper, the Washing of the Feet, the Betrayal of Judas, the Prayer of Joachim and of Anne, the Blessing of the Virgin by the Priests, the Presentation of Mary in the Temple. It is true that a few scenes from the Passion do figure in the narthex of the two other mosaic-decorated churches. But there are less of them, and as to the cycle of Childhood it occurs only at Daphni and as a forerunner of the typical development of cycles of frescoes which came later.

Before leaving these three mosaic-decorated churches of the eleventh century, both very different and very similar, we must stress their great aesthetic value, which corresponds both to an ideal of beauty and to a no less ideal form of religious thought: a harmonious balance on the one hand, a symbol of the Kingdom of God on the other. The luminous gold of the vast empty spaces which surround the figures contributes greatly to the success of the Byzantine artists in achieving this double aim.

The later development of Byzantine mosaics can only be studied outside the Byzantine lands. There exist of course a few isolated mosaic panels from the twelfth century in the cathedral of Serres — of which all that remains today are some fragments of a Communion of the Apostles which used to be in the apse and are now in the Lapidary Museum inside the rotunda of St. George in Salonika — and in the Monastery of Vatopedi on Mount Athos (an Annunciation in the narthex). The rest are in Sicily and in Venice. Consequently the best examples of Byzantine mosaics of the Comnenian period (about 1080 to about 1200) are outside Greek countries and are mainly used for the decoration of basilical churches of the Latin type. For us these mosaics must take the place of those which were created in Constantinople and elsewhere in the twelfth century, and which must have served as models to the mosaicists of Venice and Palermo, who were however helped by Italian pupils. It is very difficult to distinguish between authentic Byzantine works and their local imitations.

Mosaics in non-Byzantine countries

The oldest mosaics in St. Mark's in Venice must have been entirely Byzantine. They date back to the end of the eleventh century and are located at the entrance and in the choir of the church. Others cover the five domes and some of the vaults around the domes. They too are the work of Greek mosaicists and are spread over a great part of the twelfth century. Venetian helpers must have taken an increasing part in the execution of this very important decoration, far larger in fact than in the eleventh-century mosaic decors in Greece which we have just been studying. The architecture of St.

Mosaics in St. Mark's, Venice

Mark's certainly reminds one of the sixth-century church of the Holy Apostles in Constantinople, which was likewise built in the shape of a cross and crowned with five domes. But the mosaics at St. Mark's cannot equal those of the Holy Apostles. The Byzantine models of which they made use must have been more or less contemporary, as is confirmed by the choice of the principal subjects, the distribution of the images and the style of the paintings. Here we have a form of art which continued that of the eleventh-century mosaicists, and particularly the style of Daphni. Two of the domes of St. Mark's bear pictures of the Ascension and of Pentecost derived from figurations of the same subjects in St. Sophia in Salonika and Hosios Lucas in Phocis. The evangelical scenes arranged on the vaults which frame the central dome adopt and develop the iconographic plans and stylistic principles of the feast scenes which one finds in Greek mosaics.

It is true that on other panels and in other domes purely Byzantine elements are mixed up with motifs of Western origin, but these only add a few local touches to the total work, which belongs to the Byzantine school and reflects more truly the mosaics of the Comneni. Even much later, in the middle of the thirteenth century and during the fourteenth, the Doges of Venice were to renew their orders for Byzantine mosaics. These new works, no less interesting but of a different inspiration, were meant for the decoration of an external vestibule on the north side of the church and a chapel used for christenings. We will return to the art of these mosaics in the following chapter, devoted to the work of the Palaeologi.

Mosaic decoration in basilica of Torcello On an island close to Venice the basilica of Torcello still has two remarkable mosaic works of the same period, the eleventh and twelfth centuries. The Madonna in the apse, who rises against the gold background of the wall and the vault, bearing her Infant in her arms and with the Apostles at her feet, produces an astonishing decorative effect. The immense Last Judgement on the west wall is a little later. Its iconographic value is very great, as it is the last example of Byzantine interpretation of the Last Judgement.

At present there are in Sicily four twelfth-century churches which contain great mosaic works done by Greek artists and their pupils. These fine monuments owe their origin to the Norman kings who, although they were formidable enemies of Byzantium, imitated the *basileis* of Constantinople in everything connected with the visible signs of power: insignia, ceremonies and the luxury arts. It was in order to emulate the Byzantine emperors that they founded and richly endowed a great number of sanctuaries, some within their palace at Palermo (the Palatine Chapel) and others close to their residence (Monreale). The church at Cefalù, which has the oldest mosaics, is a little further from Palermo. Finally, the church of the Virgin known as the Martorana was founded by an admiral of the Sicilian royal fleet, who followed his sovereign's example by building a church and decorating it with mosaics in Byzantine style.

Mosaics in Sicilian churches

King Roger II built and decorated in rapid succession the church of Cefalù (1131–1148) and the Palatine Chapel (1129–1143). Monreale was founded by William II (1174–1182). Finally the Martorana, a church with a centralized Greek plan, was the work of Admiral George of Antioch in 1143.

In all these mosaic decorations an attempt was made to reproduce Byzantine models of the period: the same personages, the same scenes, the same style, but adapted to the interior of the churches which, apart from the Martorana, were quite different from Byzantine sanctuaries. Consequently the plan of the usual cycles had to be modified, and the true Byzantine schemes, which were too small, had to be completed by additions of varying size. Thus for example at Monreale, in the Palatine Chapel and in the Martorana, due to the absence of a dome, the Pantocrator was put in the vault of the apse, whereas the Virgin, whom the Byzantines always placed there, was moved to a lower row, on the wall of the apse itself. In the Martorana the arrangement of the subjects, beginning in the dome with the Pantocrator and the Angels, followed the Byzantine system more closely, because the architecture of this small church allowed the subjects to be grouped in this way. In the Palatine Chapel the subjects of the cycle of Feasts are grouped in the chevet instead of being arranged in the Byzantine way around the dome. Finally, the walls of the aisles of these basilicas of the Palatine Chapel and of Monreale and the lateral walls of Monreale were decorated with numerous narrative images drawn from both Testaments, from Genesis up to the Acts of the Apostles. Never, so far as we know, had such vast

PLATE P. 111

PLATE P. 91

schemes been treated in mosaics on the walls and vaults of medieval Byzantine churches. None of these sanctuaries were of course as large as the Sicilian basilicas, and from this point of view the Norman rulers of Sicily surpassed their models in Constantinople.

One may of course ask oneself whether, by these increases in size, the Norman kings were not betraying the aesthetic principles on which the works of their models were based. But as we are not in a position to solve questions of this type, it would be more reasonable to say that, if the uneven quality of Sicilian mosaics is due to the size of the works, it is because there was a shortage of qualified artisans. Thus in all these mosaics there are pieces of high quality and entire scenes wholly lacking in aesthetic value. Consequently these rich and decorative works are on the whole successful, their considerable size adding a new and original element to the true Byzantine versions. What was attempted in Sicily was also a more popular version of a form of art which in Byzantium remained eclectic. But these are merely details and it would be difficult to find traces of concessions made in order to achieve easy effects in the mosaics of Cefalù or the Palatine Chapel.

In the galleries of St. Sophia, the votive panels of the Comneni provide us with an isolated example of mosaics as they were treated at that period in the Byzantine capital, and I continue to attribute to the extreme end of the twelfth century the beautiful Deisis on these same galleries, which others date a century later. This remarkable work, like the frescoes of Vladimir (see below), exhibits a profound sensibility in the modelling of faces and conveys admirably an expression of sweet benevolence. This extremely human art is an attempt at a trend which was to be developed under the first Palaeologi.

MURAL PAINTING

If the kings of Sicily were able to afford extremely vast mosaic decorations, others with less money had to be content with mural paintings. This was the usual practice in Byzantine countries during the eleventh and twelfth centuries. Its advantage was that it allowed the artist to take a more direct and immediate part in the work; it also made possible cheap and rapid reproduction of the models that had been chosen. Very few eleventh-century frescoes have been preserved, the most remarkable being those at Hosios Lucas, at Ochrid and in Kiev. The first of these examples in the crypt and the nave of the conventual church is the most archaic. It consists of scenes from the Passion, which are an example of perfect linear abbreviations which give a very moving impression of certain scenes and heads.

St. Sophia at Ochrid has remarkable paintings in the choir, with figures of bishops, an Ascension in the vault, a Virgin in the apse and a few other scenes from the liturgical cycles. A lovely frieze of flying angels adds an elegant touch to this severe, but nevertheless more supple art than that of Hosios Lucas (around 1040). The frescoes at St. Sophia in Kiev are similar but less well preserved.

PLATE P. 113

It is through the twelfth-century frescoes in particular that we have a knowledge of Byzantine painting under the Comneni. Although there are fragments everywhere, the important compositions are to be found in the lands which were at that time under Byzantine influence, notably in Serbia, Russia, Georgia or the peripheral provinces of the Empire — Macedonia, Cyprus and Cappadocia. Although as a general rule we are concerned in this work only with Byzantine works proper, we must mention the frescoes of 1198–1199 in the church of St. Demetrius at Vladimir in north-eastern Russia, because of their exceptional historical and aesthetic importance. The other works in Byzantine-influenced countries will be dealt with in a special volume devoted to medieval art in Eastern Europe. On the other hand, the mural paintings in the outlying provinces of the Empire must be studied here. In Cyprus several churches were decorated in the twelfth century, but the style of these paintings shows a certain variety which can be explained by the practically simultaneous presence of local artists and of artists called in from Constantinople or from Macedonia. I particularly mention Macedonia because the style of the painting of the church of the Virgin at Arakou (1192) in Cyprus is closely related to the contemporary frescoes at Kastoria and Kurbinovo (see below) in Macedonia.

XIIth-century frescoes in Byzantine-influenced countries and peripheral provinces

The mural paintings of Cappadocia should really be considered as a form of regional art within the framework of Byzantine art in general. That is a reason for studying them in detail and then examining the ensemble of these frescoes from the ninth to the twelfth centuries inclusive (see below).

But even more than on these provincial works one would wish for information on the important paintings which served as examples for the others. In order to fulfil this role they should ideally have been located in Constantinople — decorating the palaces and sanctuaries which enjoyed the particular favour of the Comnenian emperors and their suite, such as the monasteries of the Blachernes and Pantocrator, the main imperial residences which stood in the Blachernes, and another near the church of the Forty Martyrs. But as no trace remains of twelfth-century mural paintings in Constantinople, we must content ourselves with works of exceptional quality that artists of great talent created using the same techniques outside the capital and beyond the borders of the empire. The first example of painting of this high quality is preserved near Skoplje in Yugoslav Macedonia. An inscription of the period dates the frescoes in the little church at Nerez to 1164 and informs us that it was founded by a member of the Comnenian family.

Art of Nerez The quality of the paintings at Nerez does indeed correspond to the conception we have of a masterpiece. The decoration, which is not complete, has two equally remarkable aspects. First of all one admires a gallery of expressive heads which give the impression of being faithful portraits of various saints. The artist succeeds in giving these faces an intense vitality, without forgetting that in order to honour these saintly figures it was necessary to give them an air of noble distinction. The two tendencies of this art are also apparent in the essential part of the decoration — that is to say, a series of vast scenes which fill the upper part of the walls and the vaults. A part only of these scenes has been preserved. They mainly correspond to events commemorated by the important feasts of the liturgical year: a Purification, a Transfiguration, an Entry into Jerusalem, a Birth

PLATE P. 114 of Mary and above all two scenes from the Passion — a Descent from the Cross and Pietà. One is immediately struck by the persuasive strength of this art when describing faces both young and old, and representing expressions of suffering, movement and different ethnical types. The pathetic themes of childhood and of suffering are interpreted in a particularly striking way at Nerez. This art displays great sensitivity and attempts to justify the part played by each actor in a scene. But when looking at this painting as a whole one realizes that the dominant feature of this art lies in the rhythm of the compositions reduced to a small number of strokes and blobs, where the harmony of the lines is supported by that of the colours, both being expressed with the same economy. The art of Nerez, which better than any other work informs us of Byzantine aesthetics under the Comneni, remains deeply anchored to the Byzantine tradition of expressing the irrational but also attempts to add the human themes of poignant emotion and the play of mime and familiar movements.

The second example of mural painting of equally high quality is in north-eastern Russia at Vladimir in the church of St. Demetrius, which dates from 1198–1199. It was founded by a Russian prince who was powerful enough to summon artists from Constantinople. Of the ensemble of decoration at Vladimir all that remains are various parts of a large composition of the Last Judgement. The field of possible observations is thus more limited. But the beauty of the figures — particularly of the faces — and the rhythm of the composition are in the same vein as at Nerez. It is another work belonging to the same type of art, with the emphasis here on a tenderness of expression which transforms the angels and saints into human beings full of goodwill. *Paintings in St. Demetrius, Vladimir*

However, in a period when the Constantinople painting of the Comneni produced works of the quality of Nerez and Vladimir, in Macedonia and in Cyprus it was developing in quite a different way, a purely formal one. In several churches at Kastoria from the end of the twelfth century and at the village of Kurbinovo about fifty kilometres away, dating from the same period, paintings originating from the same workshops offer us a baroque version of the art of Nerez. The latter is used as a basis for new linear developments: draperies are bunched together from piles of moving folds, figures at times recline to adapt themselves to the given surfaces, and backgrounds are filled with architectural features and curious furniture. But these modifications merely represent a 'mannerism' without a future. These are interesting examples of what certain provincial artists around 1200 made of the great art of the Comneni. PLATE P. 115

It is not, however, a 'regional school' that we are dealing with here. There were also frescoes made in Cyprus at the end of the twelfth century which are very close in inspiration (see above). Were Macedonian painters brought to work in Cyprus? It is more likely that the parallel arises from the similar interpretation given to the Comnenian style around 1200 in the Byzantine provinces.

Of the mosaics and mural paintings which have enabled us to study the essential facts of monumental painting some are in Constantinople, others in continental Greece, Sicily, Bulgaria and Yugoslavia. Except in a few points of detail, geographical distance seems to have affected neither the nature nor the qualities of the artistic works of these countries, which politically and ethnically often had very little in common. It was art on the Byzantine pattern which was practised everywhere. One of the characteristics of the spread of Byzantine art was that there never existed a 'colonial' form of art — i.e., art of an inferior quality designed for export into conquered territories, which might not have been of a sufficiently high standard for the inhabitants of the mother country. The whole Byzantine political system was opposed to this conception. The quality and 'modernism' (for the period) of the paintings which were done in distant countries make us think of what often happens nowadays when only the best is good enough for export. In many cases also, as in Sicily for example, the princes took the initiative in importing Byzantine art into their country, and did so in order to imitate the emperors of Constantinople. Thus they helped themselves by paying top prices for both materials and artists. In several countries, such as Sicily, Serbia and Russia, the financial means which these potentates had at their disposal allowed them to do this without difficulty.

One must not consider this art of the Byzantine expansion as a provincial form of art. Whether one takes this term to mean art of an inferior quality to that of the capital, or art having its own characteristics, Byzantine art for export fulfils neither of these conditions. In this connection it is right that we should ask ourselves whether the Byzantine provinces had a form of art peculiar to their own region. We are thinking this time of the Byzantine provinces proper and of the period which stretches from the end of Iconoclasm to 1204. Up to the present, a more systematic effort to distinguish between Byzantine regional schools has only been attempted for paintings in manuscripts during a part of this period (ninth–tenth century). But the absence of precise information as to the origin of the immense majority of Greek illustrated manuscripts condemns in advance all attempts of this kind (see, however, what is said below on p. 181 on the subject of Greek manuscripts in Italy).

Generally speaking, it is mural paintings, necessarily linked to a given region, which afford the best information on artistic activities in the provinces. But the number of examples preserved is insufficient to attempt regional grouping of this kind. In Constantinople and in all the Byzantine provinces of Europe the only differences which have been noted up to the present are due to chronology or to variations in the social background to which the works have been attributed with more or less veracity — for instance, by describing certain works as court art, or by calling certain psalters 'aristocratic' and other paintings 'monastic' or 'popular'. Up to the present the distinction between regional schools in the European provinces of the Byzantine Empire has not been drawn in a convincing way, and we believe for good reasons.

PROBLEM OF REGIONAL SCHOOLS

The Asiatic provinces of the empire were ravaged by Arabs and Turks and there is no longer a single painted decoration in any of the churches that were built — the existing fragments being rare and without significance. But by an incredible stroke of luck certain monastic communities, which cannot have been among the wealthiest, lived in grottoes, particularly in several valleys in the very mountainous region of Cappadocia in south-eastern Asia Minor. Monastic churches were also cut out of the rock and these indestructible troglodyte sanctuaries often still have the mural paintings with which they were originally decorated.

The paintings in the rock-cut churches of Cappadocia are sufficiently numerous to give us an idea of what painting was like in a distant Byzantine province between the ninth and the thirteenth centuries. We cannot draw any sort of general rule from the lesson of the Cappadocian paintings. But they do at least provide us with information on painting as it was practised in a certain district

Paintings in rock-cut churches of Cappadocia

which was well outside the important imperial centres and bordered on Semitic and Iranian territories, where Christian artists were very active before the conversion to Islam. Cappadocia was then a frontier country which had played an important role in the history of Christianity, and particularly in the development of theology and monasticism. It was there that the famous fathers of the Greek church, St. Gregory of Nazianzus also called the Theologian, St. Gregory of Nyssa and St. Basil all taught and where the latter formulated the basis of Byzantine monasticism. Between the time of these Cappadocian Fathers (end of the fourth and beginning of the fifth century) and that of the rock paintings centuries went by, destructive wars and invasions obliterated the memory and of course all material remains of this glorious past. The re-settlement of a great number of monastic communities around the ninth century proves that the initial Christian movement in this province had not been forgotten.

Taken as a whole, however, it is medieval art which we find in these monastic grottoes. This art has several different aspects, some older, and others more recent; whereas certain distinctive characteristics seem to belong to work done in a particular workshop or in a particular valley, other elements seem to have been imported from outside. It is all this taken together which defines the painting of the district — that is to say, a certain choice of means, of shapes and of iconographic schemes which are found there either simultaneously or successively. Regional art is characterized both by the similarities which one notes and by the possible idosyncrasies of an evolution which belongs to it alone.

In some of the rock chapels of Cappadocia (St. Basil, Archangelos etc.) the painted decoration is entirely, or very nearly entirely, aniconical: crosses and inscriptions of prayers summarize the iconographic scheme. It was correct to have related these odd paintings to descriptions of Iconoclast monuments. But the presence of a few figures of saints, however limited in number, encourages us to date these paintings to the beginning of the period which followed the end of Iconoclasm. The second group of rock paintings includes decorations with numerous iconographic images, rustic in style but sometimes graceful and always expressive. We mainly find cycles of evangelical scenes which follow each other without any dividing frames, extending in rows superimposed upon one another. The story of the childhood of Jesus and of the Passion have an important place in these historical strips, outside which we find portraits of saints enclosed in medallions or lined up along the wall. Amongst these churches we must mention Ballek Kilise, Belli Kilise, the first church of Tokal, and St. Eustace. The paintings PLATE P. 116 of Kesel Tchukur show a most original cycle of the Childhood of Mary.

The first to publish most of these frescoes, G. de Jerphanion, who owed a great deal to the advice of Gabriel Millet, must be credited with recognizing that the murals in the group were archaic works on account of their iconographic programme and style. Whereas he considered their art to be derived from alleged Syrian models, we prefer to think of them simply as ninth-, tenth- and even eleventh-century versions of the art practised in the district, whatever the sources which inspired it may have been. Among the latter there were of course the many paleo-Christian monuments of the country (one medieval painting reproduces a fourth-century epigram, the original of which had formerly been inscribed on the partition of a church in the county town of the district of Caesarea), but perhaps also models sent from Constantinople at a more recent date (e.g. the Evangelical cycle of Tokal I).

Whereas all these paintings decorate grottoes shaped like basilicas, another group of paintings is in rock churches — Tcharekle Kilise, Elmale Kilise, etc. — which imitate cubic churches with a dome such as were being built throughout the empire in the eleventh and thirteenth centuries. These reflections of the current architecture of the Middle Ages, the choice and distribution of subjects, and even their style prove to us that these decorations are later than the others and that they were influenced by the contemporary art of Constantinople. The prestige of the models which came from the Byzantine capital prevailed over earlier regional traditions, but was far from eliminating them; in style all these paintings, despite the more recent Byzantinisms which we find in them, are tied by a thousand links to older Cappadocian works.

This particularism appears strongly in the rock paintings of the valley of Peristrema. Here we of course discover reflections of all the categories of painting that we have enumerated, but we also observe — for example, at Agaç alti Kilise or Egri tasch Kilisesi — original subjects and stylistic interpretations of the usual subjects which stress the regionalism of this Cappadocian art and all that separated it from the Byzantine art of the capital and from the European provinces of the empire, which essentially copied Constantinople. Thanks to these paintings we notice that, despite surges of influence from Constantinople, the regions situated in the east of the empire followed different paths and maintained their own language. We are of course dealing with more or less rustic paintings and with a fairly modest social level, where a work of art was easily considered as possessing magic functions, where popular legends were echoed in iconography and demons were frequently represented pictorially. We are very much further removed from classic models than in Constantinople and its zone of influence, but on the other hand this Greek art of Cappadocia often has remarkable affinities with Romanesque painting, which is of course contemporary — or rather, slightly later.

EASEL PAINTING   Byzantine easel painting in the Middle Ages occupies a position midway between monumental art and the independent art of architecture. To judge by the texts and the rare monuments in churches (and I suppose palaces) of the best Byzantine period, the spectator was able to look simultaneously at mural paintings and paintings on movable bands (wood, stone, bronze, silver) which were fixed on the wall. In churches these were called icons — in other words, images of divine and saintly personages and representations

Church icons   of Christian events. It was in front of these that the faithful preferred to pray. Icons were the first to suffer from the Iconoclasts and were also the first to be replaced in the churches. Their place on the iconostases and in tabernacle frames (*proskynetaria*) put them into a more direct contact with the spectator. But at the same time their art had to harmonize with that of the monumental decor. The churches of Mount Sinai and Mount Athos, the Bargello in Florence, and the museums of Leningrad, Moscow, Skoplje and Athens possess works of this origin which date from the twelfth and thirteenth centuries. Generally speaking, however, the art of church icons was

PLATE 45 – Christ (detail). Ivory, middle of xth century. *Cabinet des Médailles, Paris. Cf. p. 188*

PLATE 46 – Gold icon of the Archangel Michael. Raised relief, enamels and incrustations, beginning of XIth century. *Treasury of St. Mark's, Venice. Cf. pp. 188, 189*

PLATE 47 – Enamelled cross of Pope Pascal 1 (detail), beginning of ixth century. *Cf. p. 190*

PLATE 48 – Gospel cover in silver gilt with enamels and incrustations, IXth century. *Marcian Library, Venice. Cf. p. 190*

162

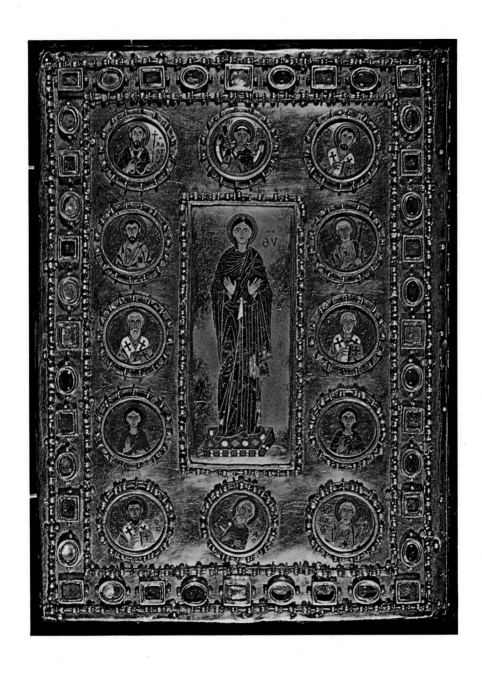

PLATE 49 – Gospel cover in silver gilt with enamels, middle of xth century. *Cf. p. 190*

PLATE 50 – Mary as a child being fondled by her parents Joachim and Anne. Mosaic at Kariye Camii, Istanbul, *ca.* 1320. *Cf. pp. 195, 198*

164

PLATE 51 – Procession of Angels celebrating the Liturgy in Heaven. Mural painting in the church of the Virgin 'Peribleptos' at Mistra (Sparta), xivth century. *Cf. p. 196*

PLATE 52 – Nativity. Mural painting in the church of the Virgin 'Peribleptos' at Mistra, xivth century. *Cf. pp. 195, 199*

166

to be even more successful under the Palaeologi and we shall return to it later.

One branch of medieval Byzantine painting remained entirely separate from monumental art. This was manuscript-painting, which was cultivated at all times with perseverance and talent by the Byzantines, who enjoyed art books and were very knowledgeable about the techniques of painting. The beginnings of this art, which was practised in the same workshops in which the manuscripts themselves were copied, go back to the first centuries of our era. In Byzantium itself the tradition started in the fourth and fifth centuries — that is to say, a period earlier than that with which this book is directly concerned. MANUSCRIPT-PAINTING

Iconoclasm had to exclude from manuscripts, as from churches, all religious images. However, the Byzantines returned very quickly to the painting of figurative subjects, probably from the time of the definite fall of the heretics in 843. Psalters illustrated with small marginal images are amongst the first works of the post-Iconoclast period. On the page of the copy owned by the Bibliothèque Nationale in Paris (MS. Grec 20) we find Christ praying at Gethsemane and (in part) Judas hanging. Sketched rapidly with light strokes, these are true and lively pictures with a frank and expressive style. *Psalters*

PLATE P. 118

In their choice and interpretation of subjects the artists who illustrated these psalters carried on the polemics of the Iconophiles in their struggle against the Iconoclasts. It is probable that this art of Orthodox propaganda was evolved in the entourage of the Patriarchs of Constantinople. The oldest copy of these psalters shows the liturgical customs of St. Sophia in Constantinople. Thus it is wrong to consider the illustration of these psalters as a monastic and popular branch of Byzantine art. An original work of this period, this illustration is realistic and direct in style, and at times verges on the vulgar, whether the motifs were newly created or borrowed many elements from a much older form of art.

The various series of paintings, which strike us on account of their elegance and the ease with which the manuscript-painters of the late ninth and early tenth centuries adapt and imitate antique models, must be considered quite differently. This is the case with a long

strip of illustrations of the Book of Joshua in the Vatican Library, a
roll of parchment unique of its kind called the 'Roll of Joshua'. This

Roll of Joshua

PLATE P. 64 is a frieze several yards long depicting successive episodes from the
victorious campaigns of Joshua. Although not directly copied, this
frieze must have been inspired by the triumph columns of the
emperors with their sculptured strips showing military subjects. The
problem that still engages the attention of specialists is to discover
whether it is an original work of the Macedonian period in which
numerous classic motifs might have been combined, or whether it
was a copy of a single Greek model. Whichever hypothesis we adopt,
these pictures, which are like light drawings, accentuated by a few
touches of colour, delight the eye. Here and there a stroke or a detail
reveals their Byzantine origin. But taken as a whole the work is
something of an anachronism and proves above all the exceptional
talent the Byzantines of that period showed in adjusting themselves
to the aesthetics of antiquity and its well-tested means of expression.
Among other manuscript paintings of similar inspiration and of
equal quality we must mention the charming pictures which dec-

Nicander's treatise

PLATE P. 42 orate a treatise on snake-bites by a Greek doctor, Nicander, in the
Bibliothèque Nationale in Paris (MS. Grec Suppl. 247). This time
we are dealing with a true copy and an example of painting faithful
to Greek taste and means of expression. As is evident from our illustration (a young man walking in the forest), one must make an
effort in order to realize that this painting was done in the tenth or
early eleventh century.

Other illustrated manuscripts from the end of the ninth century,
such as the Collected Sermons of Gregory Nazianzus (Bibliothèque
Nationale, MS. Grec 510), and of the first half of the tenth century,
such as the celebrated Psalter also in the Bibliothèque Nationale
(MS. Grec 139), or even the Vatican Bible (Reg. Gr. 1) all in their
way show the Greek painting tradition. But the second of these
famous manuscripts alone reaches perfection in its imitation of the
classical model. Another point is that all the artists who were en-
trusted with these paintings were not equally well trained for their
task. However, the best of these manuscript paintings are real
pictures enclosed in frames. Fine and noble personages with the
bearing of Greek figures are portrayed moving in a concrete space

defined by buildings and furniture. Their slow and solemn gestures convey clearly the part that the biblical subjects attributed to each of them. Certain of these scenes are famous, such as the Crossing of the Red Sea or the Combat of David and Goliath. One picturesque detail, which like nearly everything else in this art goes back to an illustration of the Psalter by an artist of the fifth and sixth centuries: the personages of biblical history are accompanied by personifications of their state of mind or of the act which they are about to accomplish. But what is particularly remarkable in this series of pictures is the pensive and at times sad or even tragic expression of the faces: King Hezekiah on his sickbed, on one of the pages we reproduce, or the   PLATE P. 88
Prophet Nathan in the scene of the Repentance of David. On   PLATE P. 136
another page are fine examples of the heads to which Byzantine art so often returned, and of which Stendhal said that they 'were lost in thoughts'.

Certain illustrations of the Paris MS. Grec 139 are also found in the Vatican Library Reg. Suev. Gr. 1, another manuscript dating from the first half of the tenth century decorated with large full-page paintings. At times the paintings of this manuscript adhere to fifth- and sixth-century models even more closely than the manuscript paintings of the Parisian Psalter; this is particularly so in the painting reproduced here, which shows Moses on Mount Sinai in two epi-   PLATE P. 135
sodes united in the same landscape. It is a remarkable fragment of painting modelled on an older work, the delicacy of the colours in the upper part of the picture being perhaps most faithful to the original. Against this one must note that the tenth-century painter was unable to capture the rapid movement of Moses receiving the Law, and that, considered as a whole, the composition does not possess to the same degree the qualities of balance and harmony that we find in the best painting of the Paris MS. Grec 139.

In the Paris MS. Grec 510 there are many illustrations of the sermons   *Basil I's copy of*
of Gregory Nazianzus. This manuscript was either ordered by Basil   *Gregory Nazianzus*
I or probably given to him a few years before his death in 885. The basis of this art is the same as that everywhere else during the reign of the first Macedonians, but as always each version had its own particularities. Here, too, old models were constantly consulted and followed, but they differed both in date and origin, and one notices

this as well as the unequal value of the artists. The cycle of images is a very broad one and includes, side by side with biblical and evangelical subjects, among them several large classical pictures, series of secular scenes which perhaps reflect illustrations by the first historians of the Church. Our plate is taken from one of the pages devoted to the history of the Christian emperors. It is probably one of the earliest known examples of the picture of Constantine PLATE P. 41 defeating Maxentius at the Milvius Bridge thanks to the intercession of Christ. In front of him, enclosed in a luminous circle, the painter put the cross with which he was to triumph, to which were added the words which according to Eusebius accompanied his vision of the cross: 'You will win in this' (in this sign).

No other manuscript gives us more information than Basil 1's copy of Gregory of Nazianzus on the iconographic background which was available in Constantinople a few decades after the end of Iconoclasm. Quite obviously the choice was based on the sermons of that great theologian, and it is quite possible that in certain cases the ninth-century painters found their models in pre-Iconoclast volumes of these same sermons. But it seems more likely to us that the illustrations of this volume copied for Basil 1 were compiled on that occasion from paintings of different origins. This is suggested on the one hand by the variations in style of the forty paintings in this volume: (a) subjects spread out in space with landscapes in depth, skies with clouds, the play of light; (b) schematic scenes, both large and small, where the entire action takes place on a single surface; (c) symbolic images which are lined up on superposed rows or inside small rectangular frames; (d) the interpretation of the human face, which varies from careful imitations of classical models as in the Paris Psalter (MS. Grec 139) to the defining of a face through a few stereotyped formulas, etc. It is of course not surprising to find that such different paintings were combined in a work which is so close in time to the Iconoclast period. What the paintings of the Paris MS. Grec 510 show within one and the same manuscript may be compared with what we see when relating to each other the illustrations in all Byzantine manuscripts of the late ninth and early tenth centuries. The variety of styles and methods shows that they must have been inspired simultaneously by ancient sources of various origins and have imitated them fairly passively.

It is only towards the end of the tenth century that we find manuscript paintings which succeeded in creating a contemporary style through the study of these models, which are invariably Greek, and nearly always bear the mark of this source. This is the true Byzantine style of the time of Constantine Porphyrogenitus and John Tzimisces. The portraits of the evangelists in two fine manuscripts — Paris MS. Grec 70 and Vienna MS. Theol. Gr. 240 — are excellent examples of the earliest version of this style. A Tetra Gospel on Mount Athos, Stravonikita, shows portraits of the evangelists of equally classical aspect and of great beauty. The 'small prophets' in a collection of the University Library at Turin are of a related style, equally classical but with a specifically Byzantine flavour.

True Byzantine style of manuscript-painting at end of Xth century

The following phase of this art is shown in certain illustrated manuscripts produced around the year 1000, and particularly in the numerous and perfect paintings of their type which are in a psalter (at the Marcian Library in Venice) and a menology (a kind of martyrology) in the Vatican Cod. Gr. 1613 — both executed for Basil II (976–1025). Preceded by a famous portrait of the emperor triumphing over the Bulgars in 1018, the paintings in the psalter comprise a series of small pictures taken from the life of David, the author of the psalms. Whereas the menology shows a great number of pictures, one on each page, recalling the events commemorated by the liturgical year, day by day and month by month, the Vatican codex only corresponds to a part of the year. The complete work was meant to cover the whole year. As to the events represented, they are episodes of the Gospels celebrated by the liturgical feasts (Nativity, Adoration of the Wise Men etc.) and death scenes — both natural decease and particularly violent martyrdom of the saints of the Church (the latter in fact combined the day of the death of the saint with his 'birth' into sanctity).

PLATE P. 137

These paintings, dating from shortly before the year 1000, must have had iconographic prototypes executed about a century earlier. They came from workshops which enjoyed a great reputation. A proof of this is that, contrary to Byzantine practice, the painter's name is written at the side of each picture. A team of painters was needed to execute the numerous illustrations of the menology. It is all the more interesting to observe that the paintings by the different artists are hardly distinguishable, whereas pictures by the same artist were no more related to each other than to other paintings in the same manuscript. We are most probably dealing here with the work of a group of artists who shared the work, while obeying the directives of a master painter.

The style of Byzantine manuscript-painting reached maturity in these paintings and in certain works of the same quality, such as the Baltimore Menology, the one in Moscow, the Mount Sinai Gospels (No. 204 and one other), one on Mount Athos, Iviron 5 and still

Characteristics of mature style of manuscript-painting another in Paris, MS. Grec 64. Here again we find the classical background of the tenth century, but strongly interpreted according to contemporary Byzantine taste. The modelling of the bodies and draperies in the Greek style is maintained, but geometrical schematization has progressed, when one compares these paintings with earlier ones. The compositions in which they are used include all the elements of the picture — human figures, architectural features and landscapes; the human figure continues to take first place, but adapts itself to the articulation of the general composition; relationships are established between the silhouettes of the figures and the edges of the mountains and the structures which rise behind them. Art now being frankly medieval, it no longer hesitates between several solutions of the problem of space; whereas a unique scale is adopted for all the figures, the third dimension, too, is translated everywhere in closely related terms. The scene takes place on a narrow strip of land, behind which rises a backcloth with buildings and landscapes; the border between the two remains rather hazy, certain figures appearing to belong at the same time to the space in front of the backcloth and to the cloth itself (thus a certain figure stands between the two hills of the backcloth but is nevertheless a personage in the foreground).

The paintings of the Paris MS. Grec 64 add luxurious ornamental decoration to the classical anthropomorphous repertory, a point we shall return to later. For the moment let us continue to examine what are properly described as paintings, and look more closely at

a remarkable aspect of the truly Byzantine work of that period —
that is to say, the careful modelling of the heads in the Greek style,
but interpreted as portraits with individual features, aquiline noses
and large expressive eyes. The ascetic ideal is beginning to assert
itself, as in the double image of Christ and the Prophet Jeremiah in a PLATE P. 65
manuscript in the Laurentian in Florence which is reproduced here.
But the voluminous forms have not yet been given up, as was to be
the case later. This is equally true of the beautiful picture of St. John
Chrysostom in the Museo Sacreo in the Vatican, also reproduced PLATE P. 184
here, and which dates from around the year 1000. The painting,
despite its monumental aspect, has the dimensions of an icon or of a
large manuscript painting; it recalls the finest style of Byzantine
painting — very classical yet with classicism interpreted in the
contemporary taste, showing a marked partiality for rhythmic composition and a certain graphism.

Towards the middle of the century a selection of the sermons of St.
John Chrysostom in the Bibliothèque Nationale (MS. Coislin 79),
preceded by portraits of Nicephorus III Botaniates (1078–1081) and
of his wife, allows us to admire other paintings in the same style
and of equally high quality. We reproduce a picture of Archangel PLATE P. 69
Gabriel which shows how classical taste persisted in regard to the
features of Gabriel's face and the quest for rhythmic composition in
the elegant figure. Here, too, graphism makes progress, particularly
in the modelling of the face and the hair. A new element (which we
will also find when we come to discuss enamels: a taste for flat
colours with vivid tints inspired by enamel colours) uses court
costume in order to adorn the archangel with a beautiful sky-blue
touch. Preoccupied by these decorative effects, the painter gives
them priority over the drapery: the archangel's blue coat with its gold
palm-leaf decoration completely hides the plastic shape of the body.

Most illustrated Byzantine manuscripts belong to the eleventh and
twelfth centuries. In view of their number it is out of the question *Illustrated Byzantine*
to describe or even mention all of them. Another point is that their *manuscripts of XIth*
art does not differ very much and the few examples we shall *and XIIth centuries*
mention will give a fairly satisfactory idea of them. However, when
mentioning the uniformity of this painting during the eleventh and
twelfth centuries we do not mean to say that all these works resemble

one another, but that in whole series of related works we see the same characteristics. This is a sign of flourishing workshops and intense activity, and seems to fit in exactly with the eleventh and twelfth centuries in Byzantium. But such a vast output obviously means that numerous workshops and a great number of artists must have been involved, both having been able to specialize in a certain type of painting and a particular style. Among the workshops whose products we know best we must particularly mention that of the monastery of Stoudion in Constantinople. In the second half of the eleventh century these artists illustrated a Tetra Gospel (Paris MS. Grec 74) which has on each page more than one graceful and brilliant picture. From this extensive collection we have chosen a PLATE P. 138 Crucifixion followed by the Dividing of Christ's Garments. This example gives us a clear idea of the refinement of this art, which mainly plays with silhouettes of figures and slender objects which stand out against the light background of the parchment, producing remarkably rhythmic compositions. Volume was entirely suppressed and the 'lights' of the draperies replaced by a network of golden streaks inspired by cloisonné enamels. From the same source originates the scale of pure and vivid colours incrusted between golden partitions.

Whereas the same art is applied in the marginal illustrations of a psalter copied in 1066 (British Museum Add. MS. 19.352), there exist counterparts to these two masterpieces from the second half of the eleventh century, several decades later, whose style and iconography are related but different. To the Tetra Gospel Paris MS. Grec 74 corresponds the Tetra Gospel Florence Laurentian VI. 23 and to the British Museum Psalter one in the Vatican, the Barberini MS. Gr. 372. Gabriel Millet contrasted the iconography of the two Tetra Gospels, which he saw as the work of epigones of the paleo-Christian schools of art, one centred on Antioch and the other on Alexandria. But there does not seem to be sufficient evidence to support this hypothesis. What does appear more certain is the more classical aspect of the two series of paintings of the Comnenian period when compared with those of the eleventh PLATE P. 139 century. Thus if the illustrator of the Laurentian VI.23 adheres to the arrangement of pictures in strips interrupting the text and to a small scale, his figures are more closely related to the classical ones than to those in the tiny scenes of the Paris MS. Grec 74. The twelfth-century illustrations go back to the typical poses of Greek figures and to their traditional draped costumes. The third dimension reappears, albeit timidly; so too do accessories, furniture and architectural forms, although foreshortened. This was indeed one aspect of Comnenian art which, without going very far in that direction, marked the beginning of a certain classic *renovatio*.

This movement is less important than that in the tenth century under the Macedonians, but it does exist, and a series of paintings and a few frescoes prove this. It seems as though the impetus of the Macedonian renaissance ceased around the middle of the eleventh century, which was also a time of troubles and political uncertainty in Byzantium. The manuscript paintings of the period of Nicephorus III Botaniates (see the Archangel on p. 69), ten years earlier than those of the British Museum Psalter dating from 1066, or of the Paris MS. Grec 74 (our plate), belong to that period which cultivated a graphic style and ornamental decor, while multiplying orientalisms. It was in the same period that Nicephorus III brought Turkish troops to Constantinople for the first time and surrounded himself with Bulgarian dignitaries. The great defeat of Mantzikert by the Seljuks (1071) was the catastrophe which brought this period to an end. The accession of the Comneni, beginning with Alexius I (1081–1118), meant the restoration of the state, and also — possibly slightly later than the political revival — a *renovatio* of the arts, which once again coincided with a new attempt at regeneration through contact with classical traditions. This revival, which lasted throughout the twelfth century, was reflected in the art of the manuscript paintings which we have just mentioned, as well as in the slightly earlier mosaics of the year 1100 at Daphni (p. 145). Considered from the point of view of a new renaissance, the Chios mosaics are related to those of Daphni, in the same way as the paintings of the Paris MS. Grec 74 are to those of Laurentian VI.23. It was during the Comnenian period, and particularly around 1100, and in the first half of the twelfth century, that a collection of sermons on the Virgin was illustrated. This work is attributed to one James, a monk at the convent of Kokkinobaphos, not far from

PLATE P. 69

PLATE P. 138

Constantinople. (Two copies are known, one in the Bibliothèque Nationale in Paris and one in the Vatican.) The same applies to the paintings which precede the beautiful Tetra Gospel of the Parma Library (Palat. 5) and which accompany a twelfth-century edition of the Sermons of Gregory of Nazianzus (Paris MS. Grec 550 and Mount Sinai). The Sinai copy originated in Constantinople at the convent of the Pantocrator, the sanctuary founded by the reigning dynasty and enjoying its patronage. Here we are probably in the presence of an art favoured by the court. Essentially this art is that of the paintings of Laurentian VI.23, but the works we have just mentioned show it in a more favourable light and in a more comprehensive fashion. The presence of Greek taste is evident everywhere, just as in Laurentian VI.23, but often this accent is even more apparent, as for example in the way the figure of St. Peter

PLATE P. 140 is constructed and draped (p. 140): scene of the Denial (Ev. Parma, Palat. 5). In all the manuscripts each painting, including the frame, is a complete picture and despite their iconographic laconism, the scenes possess astonishing dramatic intensity. This is due to the qualities of the drawing of the personages, to the preciseness of their gestures and attitudes and to the expression of their faces. This last trait is more pronounced than in earlier works; the same also applies to the structural cohesion between the different figures and the props of the scene. There is also a greater effort to define more precisely objects, architectural forms and costumes. This is also the case in the more sophisticated frescoes of the middle of the twelfth century, such as those at Nerez (see p. 114), where dramatic intensity is stressed to an even greater extent than in our group of manuscript paintings. As we have seen, the artist liked to dwell on pathetic subjects — the tenderness of children, suffering and death. We find the same tendency in our manuscript paintings: the illustrations of James' homilies spread out on a whole cycle the apocryphal episodes of Mary's childhood, whereas the paintings in the Parma Gospel dwell with emotion on the

PLATE P. 140 scenes of Christ's Passion. Our plate reproduces one of these scenes. Peter's tragic mask is skilfully contrasted with the common faces of the servants, indifferent to the drama; the brazier and the decorative loggia are shown with care. This art is animated by the same spirit as many Italian paintings of the twelfth and thirteenth centuries, which it inspired; it also heralds the Byzantine painting of the Palaeologi.

The same could be said about the paintings in several manuscripts of the first books of the Old Testament, particularly those of the Vatican (Gr. 749) and the Laurentian in Florence (Plut. v.38). This illustration of the Bible is influenced by paleo-Christian models, which seem to have been kept at a distance during the first centuries after Iconoclasm, as were all themes from the Old Testament in general (in accordance with a law of the Trullan Council in 695, which recommended the avoidance. of symbols and the 'Shadow of Truth', that is to say the biblical antetypes of Christ, since the Incarnation allows one to represent him in person). The reappearance of illustrated bibles in the twelfth century was thus a sign announcing a new period — all the more so as the art of the Palaeologi was to prolong this interest in the Bible, and was also to make use of paleo-Christian models when dealing with biblical subjects. But the style of these paintings, too, at any rate of those in the Vatican manuscript, and to a slighter degree of those in the one in Florence, shows a wish to give a new impetus to the Greek images which were being revived. This is particularly evident in the addition of new elements to their representations of men and the buildings and landscapes which surround them. The physical type of the personages varies according to the subject of the picture; when the subject demands it, scenes replace isolated figures and vast edifices take the place of a symbolical architectural motif. Technically, too, various changes take place: there is a richer form of expression; shaded and purely pictorial modelling of bodies gives them greater breadth and life; and this same increased sensitivity appears in the expression of the faces, in the preciseness of the gestures and in the care with which animals are drawn (see in particular the scene of the Creation of the Birds in the Florence Bible). One innovation which was to become important under the Palaeologi is, however, lacking: the initiation into the third dimension of volume and space. From this point of view paintings had not advanced beyond the limits laid down since the beginning of the Comnenian period.

We must also note a general tendency in manuscripts to give a larger part to ornamental decoration and thus to enrich decorative art. Whereas in the West manuscripts were covered with rich ornamental decor from very early times — the Irish and the Anglo-Saxons gave the example already in the seventh and eighth centuries — the Greeks were very slow to follow the same path. As we have said earlier, certain art critics think that the beginning of abundant ornamental decoration goes back to the Iconoclast period (726–843). But this theory cannot at present be corroborated owing to the lack of surviving manuscripts, and its historical interest is diminished because in any case it is not possible to define the role played by the Iconoclasts, due to the absence of manuscripts from that period. Another point is that the ornamental Greek manuscripts are either earlier or later than the Iconoclast period. In neither period did ornamentation ever acquire the same importance as it did in Latin manuscripts.

It was virtually only after the tenth century, particularly in the eleventh and twelfth centuries, that Byzantine manuscript-painters paid much attention to ornamental decor. From the time of the Macedonian renaissance onwards ornamental motifs sometimes appear on the frame which surrounds the picture, but quite obviously this decoration is considered as belonging to the frame itself. This point of view is typical of Greek art, which provided Byzantine painters of that period with the decorative themes of the frames (various motifs in the Paris MS. Grec 139, a complete tabernacle-frame in the Vatican Barber. Gr. 285), and not as an integral part of the painting in the manuscript, as was to become usual in the eleventh and particularly in the twelfth century. In the gospels the decoration is concentrated on the Table of Canons (table of the concordance of the four gospels) and on the first page of each gospel. In other manuscripts ornamental compositions form chapter-headings or vignettes at the beginning of a book or of a chapter. The tendency was for the artist to consider a whole page of a manuscript as a unique decorative composition, in which a part was played by each element — a vignette, a decorated capital letter, the text of the manuscript itself, with its play of down strokes and blanks, headings, accents and certain marginal signs. Often two pages visible at the same time are conceived as two panels of a decorative diptych, the paintings themselves being considered as a part of these ornamental compositions. Thus the left-hand page often shows the portrait of an evangelist in an ornamental frame, whereas the right-hand facing page combines a more or less developed vignette, an initial with or without a personage, a title in capital letters, possibly sub-titles and the text itself with its display of various signs which, although necessary for the reader, also have a decorative part to play. We reproduce the framed portrait of an PLATE P. 46 evangelist taken from a decorative ensemble of this type, an initial with figures and the ornamentation which surrounds it (Paris MS. PLATES PP. 43, 142 Grec 550), as well as two examples from a richly decorated Table of Canons (Paris MS. Grec 64).

These examples also show the two categories of motifs in use in Byzantium during the eleventh and twelfth centuries: on the one hand rugs made of rosettes set side by side with various borders and on the other marginal motifs combining tiny personages, animals and flowers, the whole at times forming little animated scenes. The theme of ornamental rugs was very successful in *Theme of* Byzantine book illustration, after having first been used in the form *ornamental rugs* of flat bas-reliefs on tympana, façades and balustrades of Christian buildings of the sixth century (St. Sophia, on the walls above the arcades) and on Muslim buildings in the eighth and ninth centuries. It is in the art of the Omayyads (the palaces of Qasr el Heir, Khirbet el Mafjar, Mchatta, and the Great Mosque at Kairouan) that we find versions of these ornamental rugs most closely related to those in Byzantine manuscript paintings of the tenth, eleventh and twelfth centuries. This type of ornamental rug probably appeared in Byzantium at the end of the Iconoclast period, at a time when the influence of early Muslim art seems to have penetrated there. This is, however, only a possibility and we must immediately think of another trend which played an important part in the elaboration of the Byzantine ornamental repertory at the end of the Iconoclast crisis.

A great many ornamental motifs that were classical and Iranian in their first origin which helped to revive Byzantine decor in the age of Justinian (first half of the sixth century), are also featured in certain tenth-century manuscripts (including the most famous, such as the Vatican Reg. Gr. 1, the Paris MS. Grec 510 and others a few decades later, as for example the Paris Coislin MS. 20 etc.), as well as in marble reliefs in the church of the Virgin of Constantine Lips (dating from 911 and also known as Fener Isa), the reliefs at Preslav, silk ornaments at Bamberg and elsewhere, or even Byzantine pottery of this period. It is in this way that the Macedonian renaissance first makes itself felt in the important field of ornamentation. From the end of the ninth century onwards themes and motifs of classical and Iranian origin, which had been in use in Constantinople as much as three centuries earlier, during the first flowering of Byzantine art, were revived. Here Iranian motifs are essential, but they may have arrived in the tenth century not directly from the East, but as part of the motifs which composed the Byzantine ornamental repertory of the sixth century. However, Muslim works which for their part made use at that period of decor of Iranian origin and which came to Byzantium through trade, may have contributed to the success of this type of ornamentation. We can be more affirmative as to the contribution of Muslim decor in regard to the theme of ornamental rugs with their rosettes and palm-leaf decoration. The Byzantine versions of this theme from the tenth century onwards are far more closely related to the Syrian Omayyad examples mentioned above than to pre-Iconoclast works such as the sculptured ornaments inside St. Sophia.

Small marginal images The other essential element of Byzantine medieval manuscript decoration — the small marginal images — are of classic origin. This is true of the graceful birds grouped around a fountain as seen PLATE P. 40 in our plate (Paris MS. Grec 64), and for the small scenes of little Negro boys hunting with children. Birds at a fountain are part of the decorative cycle of gardens cherished by Romans of the imperial period (Villa of Livia at the Prima Porta in Rome, etc.). Hunting scenes including Negro personages, the theme of children's games or that of children replacing grown-ups in scenes with wild animals or in circus games — all these subjects are 'commonplaces' of the imagery of the last centuries of antiquity. What was new was to have employed them again in the twelfth century, and to have made of these motifs — which in antiquity were in general use, also in monumental decor (mural painting, pavement mosaics) — elements of a small-scale decor reserved for manuscripts, and even exclusively for the marginal decoration of certain well-defined pages of these manuscripts. Nevertheless these entertaining little secular scenes added a new feature to manuscript decoration when they appeared in the twelfth century. The examples which have been preserved make us think of them as an innovation of the Comnenian period (the motif of birds around a fountain appeared earlier, but remained schematic before the end of the ninth century); at any rate they were only fully expressed at that time. This is also true of illuminated initials decorated with religious figurations, as well as of figures of animals, monsters and a whole cycle of motifs taken from the circus (athletes, conjurers, acrobats and trained animals). This decor based on secular subjects taken from public entertainments may be considered as of Hellenic origin, as we have just mentioned, but it seems rather to be a Byzantine invention of the Comnenian period. In the Greek manuscript it is the counterpart to the drolleries of more or less contemporary Latin monuments (from the eleventh century onwards in England and in the Bayeux Tapestry). The development of this decor should be considered as part of the renewal which one observes in many Byzantine works of the twelfth century, to whatever category they belong.

In speaking of Byzantine manuscript-painting we have only taken into account the most beautiful and the most typical ones, which were for the most part, if not entirely, conceived in Constantinople. As we have said in the introduction, it was mainly there that the works of art of the period were created or at any rate the models which were copied in the provinces.

In the vast majority of cases we have no indication as to the place of origin of illustrated manuscripts and are thus unable to pick out the provincial works or to attempt to establish their characteristics. However, like the mural paintings of Cappadocia, the illuminated manuscripts of southern Italy are an exception to this rule. We know of a group of Greek manuscripts which were copied and illustrated in Calabria and elsewhere, as at Salerno and Grotto Ferrata in southern Italy; others can be attributed to Rome, where several monasteries traditionally sheltered communities of Greek monks.

Paintings in Greek manuscripts in Italy

The most original of these illuminated manuscripts is a collection of the sermons of Gregory of Nazianzus, dating from 941 and coming from Reggio in Calabria (Patmos 33). The Pierpont Morgan Library possesses another curious manuscript decorated with miniatures (The Life of Aesop and the Fables of Bidbai, translated from the Arabic). Finally, among the Greek manuscripts which we attribute to Rome, we must mention the Gregory of Nazianzus of the Ambrosian in Milan (Ambr. 49–50), the Sacra Parallela in the Bibliothèque Nationale in Paris (MS. Grec 923) and the Book of Job in the Vatican (MS. Gr. 746). all of the ninth century.

The art of all these paintings in the Italian Greek manuscripts is not the same as in those of Constantinople. There are of course elements inherited from the paleo-Christian background, but we also find elements borrowed from more or less contemporary works from the immediate environment of the Greek painters in Italy: Carolingian, truly Italic and even Arabic. The paintings of these Greek workshops in Italy are thus on the border-line of Byzantine art proper. But the historical role of these workshops in the first flourish of medieval Italian art must have been considerable. It is sufficient to recall the paintings of the Exultet and the frescoes at Castelseprio, which one cannot imagine without their immediate Byzantine models. One day it will be possible to evaluate what Ottonian painting in Germany (tenth–eleventh centuries) owes to the experience of the Greek painters in Rome and their rivals in northern Italy. The paintings of the Book of Job in the Vatican seem to announce immediately the birth of some of the most striking paintings of the Ottonian era.

It will be noticed that the Greek art of the Middle Ages as it was practised in the outlying provinces of the empire (see our observations above on the frescoes of Cappadocia and central and southern Italian manuscript-painting) is closer to contemporary Western art, while that of the Byzantine capital takes us further away from it. Without going into a lengthy explanation of this suggestive fact, let us simply say that the relative isolation of the work of Constantinople was due to an understanding of the aesthetics of classical antiquity, which was far more profound in the Byzantine capital than anywhere else.

PLATE 53 – Christ's Miracles. Mural painting in the church of the Virgin 'Pantanassa' at Mistra, xivth century. *Cf. p. 195*

PLATE 55 – Icon of the Last Judgement (detail: Resurrection of the Dead, Weighing of Souls, Fate of Sinners). Mount Sinai, xiith century. *Cf. p. 203*

◀ PLATE 54 – St. John Chrysostom. xith-century icon on the lid of a casket. *Museo Sacro, Vatican. Cf. pp. 173, 203*

PLATE 56 – Icon of the Archangel Michael (detail), xivth century. *Byzantine Museum, Athens. Cf. p. 203*

Modern art historians have often underlined the mistake that is made in classifying as 'industrial art' medieval works of gold and silver, figurative enamels, ivory sculptures and generally speaking the works which owe an essential part of their aesthetic value either to a precious substance or to a difficult technique. The price of the material has nothing to do with aesthetic values; the technical qualities of a mosaic are just as great as those of an enamel, because of course in none of these arts did the machine ever replace the manual works of the artisan.

In other words these forms of art should be placed on the same level as painting, which was the major art of the Byzantines of the Middle Ages.

Monumental sculpture hardly existed in Byzantine countries at a time when in the West it was making enormous and lasting strides. Neither in ecclesiastical nor in secular art do we see any examples during the period we are considering, and its absence cannot be explained by legislation against it. It is just possible that the Iconoclast attacks, which sought to portray the Iconophiles as idolaters, excluded sculpture, a more 'material' form of art, from the techniques that could be used for the creation of sacred images. The rare sculptures which have been preserved (eleventh–twelfth centuries) belong to the realm of secular art — a statue in the Istanbul Museum of an acrobat walking on his arms with his legs in the air, and two or three reliefs on the bases of columns with effigies of dignitaries or barbarians. At times church art, too, attempted to adopt very elegant bas-reliefs of the Virgin or the Saints, side by side with the Triumph of Hercules and Alexander rising to heaven. These reliefs were set into the façades of churches such as St. Sophia in Kiev and St. Demetrius at Vladimir etc.; they were close to the monumental scale (consider the façades of St. Mark's in Venice) and seem to have been more numerous in the twelfth century than they were before. It is likely that this development, however limited it may have been, may have been related to the sudden flowering of monumental Romanesque sculpture. The capitals, cornices and above all iconostases of the Macedonian and Comnenian periods were frequently covered with ornamental reliefs, including zoomorphic elements: one also finds this in southern

Italy, where Byzantine influence is more evident than elsewhere in the West — although this is not the only province of the Latin world where the sculptured decoration of Byzantine furniture penetrated at the beginning of the Romanesque period.

This plastic decoration was often applied to furniture covered in bronze or silver (iconostases, canopies, frames of icons) and still more often to vases and other objects of ecclesiastical and secular use, and even to icons themselves. Nearly all the large-scale pieces have disappeared, but one can still admire smaller but equally precious works executed in this technique..A small masterpiece of this type is an image in relief (repoussé) in gold which represents PLATE P. 160 the Archangel Michael (Treasury of St. Mark's, Venice). In Byzantium, too, bronze reliefs (made by the throw-away method) were very popular. The finest examples of these are two small icons of the Virgin, one in the Victoria and Albert Museum and the other at Torcello. Other icons of the same type, and equally numerous, are made of soapstone and ivory.

Ivory objects   Ivory, a traditional luxury material, was always very popular in Byzantium, from the earliest times up to the Palaeologian era. But it is during the period we are studying that we find the greatest number of ivory objects, decorated with small elegant reliefs. In the field of secular art no series of objects is better represented than that of ivory caskets decorated with minute reliefs. Scenes and personages taken from the cycle of Dionysus and Hercules, scenes from the circus, of animals and monsters and classical ornaments form a graceful and amusing repertory. It seems that it was in the tenth century that these caskets were most often made. The ease with which Byzantine ivory-workers of that time imitated classical models was only equalled by that of the Constantinople manuscript-painters, their contemporaries. These ivory caskets are the most eloquent witnesses of the Macedonian 'renaissance'. In the eleventh century and later, without this type of work being abandoned, the style altered and became medieval.

The same technique was used in the production of small-scale reliefs with religious subjects, the most famous being triptychs with images of saints in prayer before Christ. The so-called Harbaville triptych in the Louvre and another in the Palazzo Venezia in Rome are the most beautiful in this series, whereas an isolated plaquette in the Cabinet des Médailles in Paris (middle of the tenth century) shows PLATE P. 159 Christ blessing the imperial couple Romanus II and his consort. Whereas the reliefs on caskets for secular use merely imitate models of late classical art, the ivory of Romanus II is of an original style, which having assimilated classical aesthetics uses them with complete ease in order to convey purely Christian visions. This fine ivory Christ — with the noble and serious head and the draperies of His garments — is one of the greatest successes of tenth-century Byzantine Christian humanism.

After reliefs of every type, some other aspects of Byzantine luxury arts may be mentioned. The same icon in Venice which provided us with an example of repoussé relief shows one of the particularities of the best Byzantine goldsmiths' work. This art, closely linked to effects of the glow and colour of gold, frequently combined several different materials in the same object, in order to create a symphony of different shapes, colours and tactile values. On the icon of the Archangel in Venice (see above p. 188) the total effect includes, besides the relief in gold, backgrounds lined with filigree work of incredible delicacy which form graceful ornaments, rows of pearls, *cabochon* and other incrustations of coloured stones and finally polychrome enamels with ornaments.

OTHER BYZANTINE LUXURY ARTS

PLATE P. 160

The combinations of the various techniques alter from one valuable object to another, as do the number of techniques used. Most frequently rows of pearls and enamels with ornamental motifs and personages were attached to a silver-gilt body. This is what we find on the richest of the series of tenth- and twelfth-century chalices and patens which have been preserved in the Treasury of St. Mark's. It is one of these chalices, among the most beautiful (middle of the tenth century), which we reproduce in our plate as an admirable example of Byzantine enamel work of the best period. This technique of polychrome decor had been used since antiquity, and by the Byzantines themselves since the time of Justinian in the sixth century. But it was only around the ninth century, probably due to some technical discovery, that cloisonné enamels (colours poured into minute compartments, separated by partitions perpendicular

ENAMELS

PLATE P. 68

Development of cloisonné enamel

to the base) suddenly flowered, because it became possible to vary the colours and to establish complicated networks of these partitions. From then on enamel work became a branch of figurative painting, one that was extremely successful because of the glow of the colours,

PLATES PP. 67, 161, 162, 163

which no other technique of painting was able to equal. It could be rivalled only by mosaics — and by stained glass, which the Byzantines, like the Muslims of that period, do not seem to have known, except in the form of coloured glass stuck together without figures or even decorative motifs. Thus enamels exercised a great influence on contemporary Byzantine painting and were of particular importance as regards manuscript-painting, probably in the latter half of the eleventh and in the twelfth century. Byzantine enamels always appear in the form of gold plaquettes, rarely bronze or silver, on which enamelled images are fixed. Each piece of enamel is made separately and later soldered on to a metal plaque of any size or shape and even on to materials for ceremonial dress, altar-cloths etc. Thus there were silver iconostases decorated with enamels, and two such large objects, decorated with numerous enamels as well as with *cabochon* and filigree work, still exist.

Pala d'Oro in St. Mark's, Venice

The most famous is the Pala d'Oro in St. Mark's, Venice, an altar-piece fixed behind the high altar; despite many transformations in the fourteenth century, this is a thirteenth-century work created in Venice with elements of an older altar-piece and enamels made at that period. The enamels are grouped in such a way as to form a large coherent composition: Christ in His Majesty surrounded by the Evangelists receives homage and veneration from the angels and the saints, while above him and on the sides are scenes taken from the Gospel and the story of St. Mark. The Archangel Michael and the large compositions of the top row are later than most of the other enamels and may come from the iconostases of the monastery of the Pantocrator, the sanctuary founded by the Comneni in Constantinople in the twelfth century.

The second important example of Byzantine enamel work is an eleventh-century icon in the form of a triptych which until recently belonged to the monastery of Khokhoul in Georgia and is at present in the Tbilisi Museum.

GOLD WORK Being unable to dwell at length on all the luxury techniques of the

Byzantines, we shall merely mention bronze works incrusted in silver or decorated with gilded motifs. Byzantine church doors, in Italy (Monte Sant' Angelo in Apulia, St. Paul 'outside the walls' in Rome) and at Suzdal in Russia are the best examples of works created by these very special techniques. The cutting of semi-precious stones flourished in Constantinople during the Middle Ages. The Treasury of St. Mark's possesses numerous examples in the form of bowls and dishes in malachite, onyx, serpentine, alabaster etc. The surviving examples date from the ninth and tenth to the twelfth century. This same period has left us numerous glyptic objects; small icons and brooches on which effigies of Christ, the saints and angels are engraved. The smallness of these pieces does not prevent the application to them of the noble and solemn style which the Byzantines knew how to apply to their work on any scale with infallible tact.

Cutting of semi-precious stones

Glyptics

One could end this enumeration of the techniques of the minor arts, which played an essential part in the artistic work of Byzantium before 1204, by speaking of marquetry, lustred and decorated ceramics. At present there are certified tenth- and eleventh-century pieces made by these techniques in the museums of Istanbul, Sofia, the Louvre and Baltimore. Both these techniques were used to produce fine pieces of monumental decor or were applied to the furniture and the floors of churches, as well as to small and large icons, whose colours are nearly as bright as those of enamel. The development of all these techniques of polychrome decor took place during the Macedonian renaissance.

Marquetry, lustre and decorated ceramics

It was during this period, too, that the Constantinople workshops located in the Imperial Palace, or which worked for the palace, produced very fine silks: materials decorated with various ornaments, including zoomorphic motifs and even human figures. It is fairly certain that this branch of luxury art (for once one may speak of industrial art, because the textiles in question were woven on looms) existed in Byzantium well before the Iconoclast period, and the emperors who were hostile to images of saints had no reason to put a stop to this production (see above, p. 95). But in any case we know, from surviving fragments of these materials bearing inscriptions of their origin, that under the emperors of the Macedonian

DECORATED SILKS

dynasty textiles of this type were the monopoly of the Byzantine sovereign, and that the ornaments which decorated these silks were copies of Iranian models in their contemporary or slightly earlier Muslim versions. The Macedonian renaissance did its best to encourage the classical style; and we have seen earlier the extraordinary success registered in certain imitations of the antique by Byzantine manuscript-painters and ivory-workers of that period. Nevertheless in the same period, and for the same lovers of Byzantine art, numerous ornamental decors crowded with Iranian and Muslim motifs were produced. Luxury textiles were among the scrics of objects most affected by this Oriental fashion.

However, in this field the artists knew how to combine Oriental decor with figurations of classical origin, as for example on the large textile curtain in the Treasury of Bamberg Cathedral (beginning of the eleventh century). An emperor is shown astride a white horse, a labarum in his hand, while two personifications (Rome and Constantinople offer him a crown and a helmet. Perhaps this is a picture of the Triumph of Constantine. It is in any case a revival by Byzantine imperial palace art of a triumphal theme and of a technique dating from the end of antiquity.

V. FIGURATIVE ARTS FROM THE
THIRTEENTH TO THE FIFTEENTH CENTURY

As we have said above, the figurative arts, especially religious painting, experienced a final period of greatness at the time of the Palaeologi. In spite of the political difficulties which heralded the approaching end of the Byzantine state the workshops of Greek mosaicists, painters and sculptors remained very busy, and orders were not lacking, chiefly from members of the important noble families of Constantinople and the provinces, as well as from the Slav, Bulgar and Serbian princes who followed the example of the Byzantine emperors. Most works of art of the Palaeologi are to be found in the capital of the empire, at Mistra, in the north of Greece, Serbia and Bulgaria.

We have reserved a special chapter for this late branch of Byzantine figurative art as it shows original characteristics in relation to earlier works of the same kind; this is far less true of architecture, which is why the buildings of the Palaeologian period were treated immediately after those of the preceding era.

It was in the sphere of mural painting, frescoes and mosaics that the most remarkable works were created by the Byzantine artists of this period. But before going into this more fully we should note that during this period sculpture and illustrated manuscripts were also very original and creative. At this time too, beautiful tombs of a new SCULPTURE type with sculptured *arcosolium* were made. On one funeral monument, originally in the church of Constantine Lips, restored by the wife of Michael VIII Palaeologus, busts of the young Christ and the Apostles appear. Certain of these sculptures, a little smaller than normal, are of great beauty, very individual, nervous, indeed tormented. The faces are like Byzantine versions of thirteenth-century Gothic sculptures — see, for example, the pediment of the porch on the northern façade of St. Mark's, Venice. After a first trial period, which has been little studied, in the eleventh and twelfth centuries Byzantine sculpture entered upon an era of remarkable development. This occurred at the end of the Latin period in Constantinople and probably in opposition to Latin plastic works (for example, a Gothic funeral monument in the Byzantine Museum in Athens). But this only seems to have been a single blaze with no future, as with mural paintings (see below).

MANUSCRIPT-
PAINTING
The painting of manuscripts under the Palaeologi continued a very ancient tradition, and there remain in being several large examples, some rather ordinary, such as the Gospels (Paris MS. Grec 54), and others more inspired, such as the theological works of John Cantacuzenus (Paris MS. Grec 1242). Manuscript paintings do not seem to have achieved the success that they had at the time of the Macedonian renaissance or even under the Comneni. But on the other hand the book illuminations of the Palaeologi are very varied and in some cases appear to be more independent of Byzantine tradition than all other types of artistic works. Some series of manuscript paintings are in a new style susceptible to outside influences. Thus the art of the illustrations in the Chronicle of Skylitzes from the thirteenth and fourteenth centuries (National Library, Madrid) are fairly composite. Usually they are content to repeat the type of Byzantine illustrations done in the eleventh and twelfth centuries, the period when Skylitzes could have been illustrated for the first time, but they are enriched by motifs inspired by Arabic or Turkish miniatures and perhaps by some Western elements. Unfortunately the place of origin of these precious miniatures is unknown. In Paris a medical book of 1339 (Paris MS. Grec 2243) and two manuscripts of the Book of Job also come from the Palaeologian period. But they are in no way alike: one of the Books of Job (Paris MS. Grec 134), from the thirteenth century, shows evidence of contact with contemporary Arabic paintings — for example, the illustrations of Kalila and Dimna, which the Greeks had copied since the tenth century at Salerno (see above, p. 182). The second copy of the Paris Job (MS. Grec 135) is dated 1368 and must have been copied at Mistra. It is all the more interesting to note that the art of these illustrations entirely follows the Gothic models of the period, probably the illustrations of northern Italy or central Europe. Although they are in a canonical book of the Bible, these paintings have an entirely secular aspect. Generally it is secular and princely art, and religious art in those

aspects closest to secular art, which in Byzantium under the Palaeologi departs more often and more easily from the ancient Byzantine tradition.

The religious paintings which decorate the walls of churches, on the other hand, remained faithful to this tradition. But this basic traditionalism did not prevent the Byzantines from creating a new version of this religious art. Its originality is shown in the series of mural decorations, in the iconographic interpretation of themes, and above all in style — that is to say, in the art itself. Leaving aside the problems of how this art was revived and the sources that inspired its creators, let us consider the works themselves.

RELIGIOUS MURAL PAINTING

In the forefront come several masterpieces which show the technical ability of the artists and in consequence the level at which the best of these paintings should be placed. Disregarding chronology, let us quote the mosaics in the two vestibules of the monastery of the Chora (Kariye Camii) in Constantinople and the frescoes in a chapel added to the same church (about 1315–1320); the mural paintings in the church of Sopočani near Novibazar (Serbia) about 1265, and the mural paintings in the church of the Virgin Peribleptos at Mistra (the ancient Sparta) towards the middle of the fourteenth century. PLATE P. 166
There are several other decorations in mosaic in the same style in Constantinople, in Thessalonica, at Arta, in Venice and in dozens of churches with painted walls and vaults from the thirteenth to the middle of the fifteenth century. Of those dating from the thirteenth century we may note Mileševo (Serbia, around 1240), Boiana (Bulgaria, 1259), St. Clement's at Ochrid (Macedonia, 1295), and of the fourteenth-century ones that known as the Metropolis, the Brontocheion (Aphentiko) and the Pantanassa Virgin at Mistra; PLATE P. 183
also Kastoria, Prizren, Staro-Nagoričino, Gračanica, Lesnovo and a series of others in Macedonia and Serbia (from various dates in the fourteenth century).

After the Byzantine mosaics and paintings of the preceding period all these works strike one by the increased number of pictures placed close together, by the greater density of figuration on each panel, and by the constant effort to portray volume and space. An iconographic and religious programme far vaster than ever before in Byzantium corresponds to these general tendencies in decorative effect. Without forsaking pictures of events of the great religious feasts and portraits of the saints, other events inspired by the Gospels were added, such as the Childhood of Christ, His Passion, miracles PLATE P. 164 and parables. In the case of Mary's partly apocryphal life they went no further than the story of her youth and the events surrounding her Assumption. As well as these cycles of events there are paintings of the lives of saints, patrons of the church and sometimes of all the saints of the calendar. Also shown were the oecumenical and other councils which reminded the faithful of the creed of Orthodoxy and the struggle against heresy. But the most interesting innovations do more than just increase the number of subjects; they tend to reflect directly the eucharistic rites celebrated in each church. Thus one finds pictures which show, with surprising mystic realism, the Infant Jesus laid out on the paten and sometimes, leaning over Him and officiating, saintly bishops who seem to be touching His body with their stylets (the instrument used by priests to set apart the pieces of bread for communion). Other painters PLATE P. 165 show Christ and the angels celebrating mass, a reminder of the Byzantine doctrine that worship on earth was only a reflection of that being rendered perpetually by the angels to God in heaven. Elsewhere different objects from the Old Testament are shown, which the Greek Fathers considered amongst the antetypes of the Virgin: the Burning Bush, the Ark of the Covenant etc. The Byzantine iconographers of this late period themselves created, or at least transferred on to the walls of churches, typological pictures of this kind, a great number of which throw light on the dogma of the Virgin Mother of God and through her that of the Incarnation, the sacrament of communion, and so once again the liturgy celebrated in the Church. Contrary to the principle that the Byzantine Church had observed since the end of the seventh century (Trullan Council, 695) biblical subjects come back again, and are fairly numerous in mural painting. They include the theophanic vision of the prophets which allows the iconographers to show God in Heaven, the Logos apart from the Incarnation — in the Divine Wisdom. By definition it is invisible, but it might be thought possible to suggest its appearance as it revealed itself momentarily to the prophets. Lastly, in another breach with the customs of

Byzantine church decoration, religious allegories are seen again (the Lamb, personification of the Virtues, the Well of Knowledge, Fathers of the Church inspired by God, the Tree of Jesse), and the faithful themselves are shown in devotion, as well as the donors in prayer, more numerous than before, crowds of Christians in front of icons singing hymns to the Virgin, and much else besides.

It is certainly not easy — nor would it be useful — to summarize briefly all the innovations in mural painting under the Palaeologi. But two or three tendencies are evident: first, the intention to make of the church a sort of illustrated book to instruct the faithful in all that might concern their faith. The accent here is placed on the liturgy, but the decoration as a whole goes much further. In a more modest fashion it is a method which reminds one of the façades and stained-glass windows of Gothic cathedrals which E. Mâle sees as an encyclopedic mirror. This monumental imagery in Byzantium is a counterpart to that of the West, exactly in the same way as the great funeral sculptured monuments mentioned above are counterparts to the sepulchral monuments of the feudal society of the West. In both cases it is a question of Byzantine responses to Western works and not of influence (except in manuscript paintings, which are sometimes said to imitate frankly Western models).

Conception of church as illustrated book to teach the faithful

An examination of the forms of Palaeologian painting gives some idea of the sources used by the Greek artists. First of all we must enumerate all those which they normally found in the paintings of their immediate predecessors, the painters of the twelfth century. As has already been said, few of the mural paintings of this period have been preserved; but by adding to them the manuscript paintings of the twelfth century one realizes that the century of the Comneni was very fertile in artistic inventions of all kinds, which in part heralded the paintings of the Palaeologi. It was then that some of the iconographic forms which we have just quoted were created — forms which one already tends to associate with the art of the Palaeologi, especially in its earliest phase: the moving treatment of such themes as the Virgin and Child, suffering, mourning, or even the delicate beauty of angels' faces.

Sources which inspired Greek artists

Thus crowds began to be represented and increased use was made of realistic additions and architectural backgrounds. In the second half of the twelfth century the mosaics in Sicily, a reflection of the art of Constantinople under the Comneni, opened the way for two typical characteristics of Palaeologian painting: detailed narrative cycles and the installing in the corridors of buildings of scenes deployed in space and depth. At the beginning of the thirteenth century — that is to say, during the Latin Empire in Constantinople — other sources of inspiration were brought into play, which probably affected painters in the capital and those who, having perhaps left Constantinople, had rejoined the Greek government set up at Nicaea, as well as those in the houses of other Orthodox princes. Due to the lack of monumental paintings remaining in these towns, one can only put forward hypotheses. But the frescoes at Mileševo (around 1240), at Boiana (1259) and particularly at Sopočani (around 1265) prove that most characteristics of Palaeologian painting can only have been formed at the time of the Latin Empire. Certainly one could imagine that the Byzantine artists must have developed during their stay in Bulgaria and Serbia; but this hypothesis must be excluded as it is a question here of deep influences and beautiful adaptations of old mosaics and paintings that were Greek in taste and feeling. Thus inspiration of this kind had a greater chance to influence painters in a large Greek city which was filled with ancient monuments and had traditionally sheltered artists' studios. In practice one can only think of Constantinople or Thessalonica, without excluding either, but insisting on the great success in imitating the classical in these frescoes, especially at Sopočani (but also in St. Clement's at Ochrid in 1295 etc.): without a background of classical culture and the traditional admiration for the antique it is impossible to imagine that they should be so complete, with their drawings of buildings, their volume and foreshortenings, the majestic personages nobly draped in togas etc.

It is here also that there is gradually to be seen in the mural paintings of the thirteenth century the development of another typical feature of Palaeologian painting, the resort to a style of large thick strokes and the use of blobs, which replace the graphic methods and fine strokes of Comnenian mural paintings. From the middle of the thirteenth century onwards virtually every characteristic feature of Palaeologian painting was foreshadowed or outlined.

However, more emphasis should be laid on the ease with which the painters of Palaeologian times, heirs to a long line of experts engaged in the same task, allowed themselves to be inspired by models from all ages. The early critics of Palaeologian painting, who knew only of isolated works (chiefly the mosaics of Kariye Camii)' took PLATE P. 164 them for copies of paleo-Christian Syrian paintings. Such a theory would find no support today, in the face of an abundance of Palaeologian works which have no connection with ancient Syrian art, but obviously revive methods and motifs of classical origin. As against the mosaics of Kariye Camii, the frescoes of the Peribleptos at Mistra and others make a particularly striking impression, as PLATE P. 166 here the various picturesque motifs owe their inspiration to early Christian art. Thus one finds beneath evangelical scenes, but having little or no connection with them, a stream with wading birds, beautiful peacocks or scenes of children at play. To find motifs of this type the painters of the fourteenth century had no need to go back to pagan works; the Christian mosaics of late antiquity (the dome of St. Constanza in Rome) offered other examples of this. We are in a position to quote examples of direct inspiration by a fifth-century mosaic (that of Christ Latomos in Thessalonica, which inspired a fourteenth-century icon now in the Sofia Museum); by seventh-century mosaics — compare the figures and the mosaic bases at St. Demetrius at Salonika or a work similar to the frescoes of Mileševo, with large figures on a background imitating gold cubes; by mosaics of the eleventh century — compare the faces on the mosaics of Hosios Lucas in Phocis with heads in fourteenth-century paintings in Macedonia; by numerous models of the sixth century — compare the throne of the Virgin at Staro-Nagoričino and the thrones of the consuls on ivory diptychs; and lastly by twelfth-century illuminations — for example, the fourteenth-century biblical theophanies in St. Clement's at Ochrid, which are modelled on certain illustrations of the sermons of St. Gregory of Nazianzus by the painters of Comnenian times. In many cases one hesitates between the influence of paleo-Christian mural paintings and of the Romanesque frescoes in Latin countries, as in the case of the motifs of ornamental medallions on the summit of a fourteenth-century calotte or arch at Kariye Camii and the Holy Apostles at

Salonika and elsewhere and on the other hand the paleo-Christian dome at Bagawat (fifth century), the Romanesque dome of Lambach in Antioch, and the thirteenth-century calottes in the vestibule of St. Mark's in Venice.

Contacts with the West The last point of comparison reminds us that Palaeologian painting flourished during a period of great development in European art, of which the contemporary Byzantine artists must have been aware. Some of the first critics of Palaeologian art considered it to be a Byzantine reflection of Italian models, claiming correctly that the Italian paintings of the Dugento and the beginning of the Trecento have many points in common with contemporary Greek works. But exactly as with the 'Syrian' theory, this 'Western' theory was advanced at a time when only a small number of Palaeologian paintings were known, and in particular when no one knew of the frescoes in Palaeologian style from the thirteenth century, the time when the new style first appeared. Now two things seem to be established; first that the origin of Greek and Italian works of this period — particularly those of the twelfth and thirteenth centuries — spring from a common base of forms and experiments which go back to twelfth-century Byzantine art; an art which in Italy found a fertile field for development. At this period and right up to the middle of the fourteenth century points of contact and interdependence are not lacking, as is proved by the sculptures and by the secular and semi-secular manuscript paintings quoted at the beginning of this chapter, which eloquently show how contemporary Western art penetrated into the works of the Greek studios. This also applies to gold and silver work and other luxury crafts. There even exist religious paintings of the thirteenth and fourteenth centuries in which Western contributions are certain — costumes and various objects at Boiana (1259); apocryphal scenes of the preparation of nails for Golgotha at Zemen (after 1350). There can be no doubt about the contacts with Western art, nor even about the influence which it exerted on certain works in Byzantine countries; and nothing is less surprising, given the blossoming of art at this time in Western Europe and the deep penetration of Westerners into the Byzantine countries after 1204.

But nevertheless Palaeologian religious painting is not explained solely by the influence of Western art. In order to understand better its essential features and the innovations it made, it is necessary to quote the second of the opinions to which we at present adhere with certainty: that the painting of the Palaeologi developed to a certain extent independently of contemporary Western art. Suffice it to say here that, as opposed to Italian painting, from the middle of the thirteenth century onwards it had a pictorial language largely inspired by classical models and was at the same time capable of imitating nature and of creating a new monumental art. Later this art did not develop in the same direction as that of Italy, by gradually improving this imitation of nature. Shortly after 1300, at the time of Giotto's great success, Byzantine painting slowed down and then put an end to the enquiries that led to works such as Sopočani, and even to St. Clement in Ochrid, thirty years later than Sopočani and already less lively. The mosaics of Kariye Camii, the frescoes of Brontocheion and above all those of the Peribleptos at Mistra show the extraordinary skill of the artists and their loyalty to all the traditions accumulated in the workshops of Constantinople, but one sees very clearly from the elegance and decorative effect, from the virtuosity of the drawing, and from the rich and refined agreement of the colours, which seem to have been carried out in these workshops, that the innovating and robust art which first appeared in the second half of the thirteenth century was gradually giving way to a new academism, a precious art for distinguished patrons — the humanistic noblemen of Byzantium. Afterwards this academism asserted itself even more strongly; the paintings from the middle of the fourteenth to the middle of the fifteenth century, very numerous in the Balkan countries, are true witnesses to this fact. The achievements of the first decades of the Palaeologi were so rich in new creations and in the revival of older models that several generations of artisans were able to make from them very satisfactory works, sometimes of remarkable decorative effect and cleverness which lack neither variety in style nor new details. At Mistra the church of the Pantanassa is one of the last masterpieces, preceded by Gračanica, Dečani, Lesnovo and finally Kalenič in Yugoslavia, the latter directly inspired by Kariye Camii. Certain painters of the second half of the fourteenth century, such as the author of the

Essential independence of Palaeologian painting from the West

frescoes in the rock church at Ivanovo in Bulgaria, give the idea of more pronounced individuality, of the painter trying to bring something new to an art which itself apparently forbad all connection with life.

Influence of Hesychast monks on painting
Although not certain, it is probable that the remarkable growth and rapid progress of Byzantine painting toward the end of the thirteenth century was slowed down and then stopped by the influence of the Byzantine clergy and above all by the so-called 'Hesychast' monks. Whereas their opponents, who had remained more open to the example of the humanists and theologians of the West, had reason to favour a kind of 'nominalism', and as a result an art which reflected nature and the visible appearance of things, the Hesychasts were at the same time more 'realistic' — that is to say, preoccupied by the sole irrational reality of divine things, and more attached to a national past, so that they could have had reasons for wanting to exclude from religious art all that differed from this 'reality'. The triumph of these rigid monks towards the middle of the fourteenth century coincides, and probably not by chance, with the definite installation of a religious art which remains remarkable for its continued ability to apply the formulas of its great past with method and respect, but which with time becomes more and more engulfed in routine.

EASEL PAINTING

Development of icon-painting
It was during the Palaeologian period that easel painting blossomed in Byzantium. It continued to flourish under Turkish domination. These pictures used the same colours as mural paintings, but employed white of egg as a fixative instead of tannin. The production of icons increased at this period, due to the new custom of installing at least two rows of icons on the partition which separates the choir from the nave in every church and is called the iconostasis or templon; for up to the thirteenth century movable icons were probably not to be found there. One can imagine the impetus that this reform must have given to the painting of icons, as every church required them. The iconostasis icons are of two different sizes — the bigger ones on the lower half of the partition show Christ, the Virgin with Child, and the patron saint of the church concerned; the smaller ones hang above the former and generally show the feasts of the liturgical year, the Deisis, and less often the life of the patron saint. Some surviving

examples of these icons date from the tenth and eleventh centuries, but before the thirteenth and fourteenth centuries they are rare. We reproduce here a rare example of an eleventh-century icon, PLATE P. 184 painted on the lid of a wooden reliquary, which shows St. John Chrysostom.

The most important series of paintings of this type are preserved on Mount Sinai, in the churches of Ochrid, lately transferred to the museum of Skoplje, in various convents on Mount Athos and in the museums of Athens, Moscow and Leningrad.

Just as the icons vary in size from large-scale paintings to those in manuscripts, so their art oscillates technically and aesthetically between the two types of painting. The examples illustrated here have been chosen to present the two types — on the one hand the large paintings of the Virgin and the patron saints of a church which PLATE P. 186 have an entirely monumental air, and on the other hand small-scale descriptive paintings. As an example of the latter we have taken the details of a Last Judgement at Mount Sinai, which could easily be PLATE P. 185 taken for a fragment of a manuscript painting.

APPENDIX

CHRONOLOGICAL TABLE

300   Foundation of Constantinople by the Emperor Constantine (330).
Roman Empire of the East, with Constantinople as its capital, separates itself from Western Empire after the death of Theodosius I (395).

500   Reign of Justinian I (527–565).
Byzantine Empire loses a part of the Balkan peninsula, colonized by Slavs (vith century). (From the ixth century part of these territories were regained; at the same period there was a gradual conversion of the Slavs to Christianity.)

600   After embracing Islam, the Arabs seize Egypt, Syria and northern Mesopotamia from the Byzantine Empire (about 640–750).
For their part, the Bulgarians instal themselves at the gates of Byzantium (viith to xth century).

700   Iconoclast government in Byzantium (726–843), with an interval between 780 and 813.
Seventh Oecumenical Council of the Universal Church, held at Nicaea on the outskirts of Constantinople, re-establishes the use and worship of religious images (787).

800   Macedonian dynasty (867–1056).
Temporary reconquest from the Arabs of certain eastern provinces of the empire: northern Syria, Palestine (end of ixth to middle of xth century).

1000   Triumph of Byzantines over Bulgarians; destruction of their state (1017).
Separation of Latin (Catholic) Church of Rome from Greek (Orthodox) Church of Constantinople (1054).
Loss by Byzantine Empire of a great part of Asia Minor, following crushing victory by Seljuk Turks at Mantzikert (1071).
Comnenian dynasty (1081–1185).

1100   Angelus dynasty (1185–1204).

1200   Sack of Constantinople by armies of the Fourth Crusade (1204).
Latin Empire of Constantinople (1204–1261).
Foundation of autonomous Greek state of Trebizond (1204).
Greek mainland and the Aegean islands largely under the sovereignty of Franks, Italians and Catalans (from 1204).
Restoration of Byzantine power in Constantinople (1261).
Palaeologian dynasty (1261–1453).

1400   Byzantine despotate of Morea (Peloponnese) with Mistra as capital (middle of xivth century to 1460).
New impetus and conquests in Byzantine territory by states of Serbia and Bulgaria (end of xiith to second half of xivth century).
Osmanli Turks progressively take over the Byzantine and Slav possessions in Balkans and Asia Minor (1350–1402).
Turks take Constantinople by assault (1453).
End of Byzantine Empire.

HISTORY AND CIVILIZATION

Baynes, N. H. and Moss, H. St. L. B. (eds.), Byzantium: an Introduction to East Roman Civilization (Oxford 1953).

Bréhier, L., Le monde byzantin, 3 vols. (Paris 1947–50).

Ebersolt, J., Constantinople: recueil d'études d'archéologie et d'histoire (Paris 1951).

Haussig, H. W., Kulturgeschichte von Byzanz (Stuttgart 1959).

Hussey, J. M., Church and Learning in the Byzantine Empire (Oxford 1937).

Ostrogorsky, G., History of the Byzantine State (Oxford 1956).

Rice, D. T., The Byzantines (London 1962).

Vasiliev, A. A., History of the Byzantine Empire, 324–1453 (Madison, Wis. 1952).

ART: GENERAL

Studies:

Ainalov, D. V., The Hellenistic Origins of Byzantine Art (New Brunswick, N.J. 1961).

Beckwith, J., The Art of Constantinople (London 1961).

Dalton, O. M., Byzantine Art and Archaeology (Oxford 1911; reprint New York 1961).

Dalton, O. M., East Christian Art (Oxford 1925).

Diehl, Ch., Manuel d'art byzantin (Paris 1910; 2nd ed. 1925–26).

Grabar, A., L'Empereur dans l'art byzantin (Paris 1936).

Huyghe, R. (ed.), Larousse Encyclopedia of Byzantine and Medieval Art (London 1963).

Mathew, G., Byzantine Aesthetics (London 1963).

Millet, G., L'Art byzantin chez les Slaves (Paris 1930 ff.).

Millet, G., Recherches sur l'iconographie de l'Evangile (Paris 1916).

Rice, D. T., Art of the Byzantine Era (London 1963).

Rice, D. T., The Beginnings of Christian Art (London 1957).

Rice, D. T., Byzantine Art (Harmondsworth 1935; rev. ed. 1954).

Wulff, O., Altchristliche und byzantinische Kunst, 2 vols. (Berlin 1914–18).

Plates:

Rice, D. T. and Hirmer, M., The Art of Byzantium (London 1959).

Volbach, W. F., Salles, G. and Duthuit, G., L'Art byzantin (Paris 1931).

ARCHITECTURE

Studies:

Choisy, A., L'art de bâtir chez les Byzantins (Paris 1883).

Ebersolt, J., Monuments d'architecture byzantine (Paris 1934).

Hamilton, J. A., Byzantine Architecture and Decoration (London 1933; 2nd ed. 1956).

Millet, G., L'Ecole grecque dans l'architecture byzantine (Paris 1916).

Plates:

Diehl, Ch. et al., Les monuments chrétiens de Salonique (Paris 1918 ff.).

Ebersolt, J. and Thiers, A., Les églises de Constantinople (Paris 1913).

Millet, G., Mistra (Paris 1910).

Millingen, A. van, Byzantine Churches in Constantinople (London 1912).

MOSAICS AND PAINTINGS

General Studies:

Demus, O., Byzantine Mosaic Decoration (London 1948).

Grabar, A., Byzantine Painting (Geneva 1953).

Lazarev, V. N., Histoire de la peinture byzantine, 2 vols. (Moscow 1947).

Monographs:

Bellew, P. and Schutz, A., Greece: Byzantine Mosaics (UNESCO World Art series, Paris 1959).

Buchtahl, H., The Miniatures of the Paris Psalter (London 1938).

Demus, O., The Mosaics of Norman Sicily (London 1929).

Diez, E. and Demus, O., Byzantine Mosaics in Greece: Hosios Lucas and Daphni (Cambridge, Mass. 1931).

Ebersolt, J., La miniature byzantine (Paris 1926).

Felicetti-Liebenfels, W., Geschichte der byzantinischen Ikonenmalerei (Lausanne 1956).

Jerphanion, G. de, Les églises rupestres de Cappadoce, 5 vols. (Paris 1925 ff.).

Kitzinger, E., The Mosaics of Monreale (Palermo 1961).

Millet, G., Le monastère de Daphni (Paris 1899).

Schmit, Th., Kahrie Djami (Sofia 1906).

Sotirou, G. and M., Icones du Mont-Sinai (Athens 1956).

Underwood, P.A., The Frescoes in the Karye Camii, in: Dumbarton Oaks Papers, vol. 9–10 et seq. (1955 ff.).

Weitzmann, K., Die byzantinische Buchmalerei des ix. und x. Jahrhunderts (Berlin 1934).

Weitzmann, K., Geistliche Grundlagen und Werke der Makedonischen Renaissance (Cologne 1963).

Whittemore, Th., The Mosaics of St. Sophia at Istanbul, 4 vols. (Oxford 1933-52).

SCULPTURE

Bréhier, L., La sculpture (byzantine) et les arts mineurs (Paris 1934).

Goldschmidt, A. and Weitzmann, K., Die Elfenbeinskulpturen des x. bis xiii. Jahrhunderts, 2 vols. (Berlin 1931).

Grabar, A., Sculptures byzantines de Constantinople (Paris 1963).

ORNAMENTAL ARTS

General Works:

Ebersolt, J., Les arts somptuaires de Byzance (Paris 1923).

Grabar, A., Le succès des arts orientaux à la cour byzantine sous les Macédoniens, in: Münchner Jahrbuch der Bildenden Kunst, ii (1951).

Kondakov, N. P., Les monuments de l'Athos (St.-Petersburg 1906).

Various Techniques:

Falke, O. von, Kunstgeschichte der Seidenweberei (Tübingen, n.d.).

Kondakov, N. P., Histoire et monuments des émaux byzantins (Frankfurt-on-Main 1892).

Millet, G., Broderies religieuses de style byzantin (Paris 1939 ff.).

Pasini, A., Il Tresoro di San Marco (Venice 1886).

Rosenberg, A., Zellenschmelz (Frankfurt-on-Main 1920).

APPENDIX OF PLATES

The appendix of plates contains the following reproductions:

1

2

3

4

5

6

7

8

214

10

11

12

13

14

INDEX

The numerals in italics refer to the plates and figures.